GW00727916

Born in Tunis and brought to London, England with her two siblings by her parents. Convent educated and passing her exams, she worked temping as a typist. Got married and moved to Kent where she had two children and later settled in West Sussex for nearly 20 years. With the children married, she eventually was forced to give up work to care for both sets of parents. When all the parents had passed away her husband was diagnosed with Parkinson's, she moved them to Dorset. She was widowed six years later and it is in Dorset where she still lives.

I dedicate this book to all the health professionals who spurred me on to write about my life and to my two children for giving me the purpose to not give up in life.

Nicole Lumiere

RECOLLECTIONS

AUSTIN MACAULEY PUBLISHERS™

LONDON · CAMBRIDGE · NEW YORK · SHARJAH

Copyright © Nicole Lumiere 2022

The right of Nicole Lumiere to be identified as the author of this work has been asserted by the author in accordance with sections 77 and 78 of the Copyright, Designs and Patents Act 1988.

All rights reserved. No part of this publication may be reproduced, stored in a retrieval system, or transmitted in any form or by any means, electronic, mechanical, photocopying, recording, or otherwise, without the prior permission of the publishers.

Any person who commits any unauthorised act in relation to this publication may be liable to criminal prosecution and civil claims for damages.

All of the events in this memoir are true to the best of author's memory. The views expressed in this memoir are solely those of the author.

A CIP catalogue record for this title is available from the British Library.

ISBN 9781398442641 (Paperback)
ISBN 9781398442658 (ePub e-book)

www.austinmacauley.com

First Published 2022
Austin Macauley Publishers Ltd®
1 Canada Square
Canary Wharf
London
E14 5AA

If anyone had said to me that I would be writing a book and it was going to be published, I would have laughed and laughed. I have always believed that opportunities like that happen to people who have great knowledge and are confident and sure of themselves.

Upper most in my mind, I thank my Angels and by saying that word I know that I am thanking my three darling tiny baby brothers my Mum miscarried very early. I know also that all my family members including my 'boys' who have passed away and are all now Angels, will have been with me in my darkest times.

Although I only ever remember reading three books in my lifetime, Space Clearing by Karen Kingston, The Wheel of Life by Elisabeth Kubler-Ross and In the Meantime by Jyanla Vanzant. I only remember them for the dramatic, positive and lasting impact they made on my life. I have also sought guidance from my Angel cards by Doreen Virtue and The Fung Shui Bible by Simon Brown. They have all contributed to my balanced and peaceful outlook on life.

Table of Contents

At this moment in time, with all the worries of the COVID-19 virus, life for me is quite lonely and has made it more encouraging for me to write about my recollections, some of which are very painful. I shall imagine that we are a group of friends having a chat over a cup of tea, and there is no virus. I hope that's ok with you.

Over the years, I was encouraged by various professional bodies to write about my experiences. The first was a health care worker at my mum and dad's surgery who had been amazed at what kind of life I'd experienced up till then. Then when we moved again, the carer's coordinator told me the same thing. Even friends suggested that I should seriously consider writing one, but in all those times, I was still very busy looking after my family members.

I remember some of their comments like 'wow, why don't you write a book' or 'you should write a book'; really what delayed it was that I didn't think I had anything special to tell and now as I said, with my being isolated from everyone because of the virus I thought I should give it a go. No that's only a half-truth.

The thing that really 'pushed me', 'kicked me up the backside' so to speak, to write my recollections were my Angel cards. I have been taking guidance from them for the last 25 years. I call them my earthly guiding Angels. These are *Angel Tarot Cards* by Doreen Virtue and Radleigh Valentine. Please don't be put off by the word 'Tarot', I don't really understand Tarot cards although I have tried, but these really are so magical, well for me at any rate.

I must share this little story with you first. When I entered my local book shop to look for these Angel cards as had been advertised in my psychic magazine, I couldn't find them, and my heart sank. I asked the assistant for help, and she took me around the corner from where I had been standing and pointed to the shelf and the array of boxed cards on offer. Taking my hand along the shelf and skimming the titles with my fingers, I felt a tingle on my fingertips and looked at the box my hand had rested on, and they were the ones I was looking for.

I pulled out the boxed cards and instantly started to cry. I felt happy, warm and overwhelmed. I knew that I was meant to have them and that they were going to be good for me. It has made me quite emotional telling you. I must say in all the years I've used different Angel cards but never as accurate as these.

Where was I? Oh yes, for the past 18 months, one card, in particular, kept coming up and it said: 'you are missing an opportunity, and it is staring you in the face'. I would say to the card: 'you keep telling me this, but I am too stupid to know what you mean. Can you enlighten me?' Well, this had baffled me in all that time, and suddenly, I got a 'light bulb' moment. Do you ever get those? Well, I did, and I was so annoyed at myself for taking so long for the penny to drop that I smacked my arm repeatedly, asking myself if my brain had been on holiday for all those months.

Of course, the missed opportunity was writing the book, and the thing that was staring me in the face was my computer screen. What a wombat was I then?

I am ashamed to say that I have only ever read three books in my life, and all of them had an extremely positive impact on me.

The first *Space Clearing* by Karen Kingston when I was in my 30s and practising 'Feng Shui', which is the art of harmonising the space we live in and certain directions we face at home and work and how these, in turn, would have a negative or positive influence on our lives. Karen's book helped me to clear out things that I thought were important in my life but were actually holding me back in my work and also affecting my health and maybe even those living with me.

About ten years later, I read *Wheel of Life* by Elisabeth Kübler-Ross. I had bought the book after watching Elisabeth on the Oprah Winfrey show, and at the time, she was in her final days on this earth. The interview was taking place with Elisabeth in her bed at her home. She was saying to Oprah that she couldn't wait for God to take her as she knew that she had experienced on earth all she needed to, and she was so excited about 'moving on', as she believed that this was not the end. Elisabeth was so inspirational in the interview and more so in her book.

The third book was sent to me by my daughter, I was by now in my early 60s, and my husband had passed away around eight months before. I was struggling to find who I was as a person and how was I going to come out of the shadows and think of myself properly for the first time in my life. The book was called *In the Meantime: Finding Yourself and the Love You Want* by Iyanla Vanzant.

I bet you're thinking to yourselves why on earth was I contemplating such thoughts so close to losing my husband? When you have finished reading my recollections, then you can make up your mind. I am not telling you so I can be judged but to show that no matter what we have to face, and put up with in life, we must always have faith in ourselves and the ones who guide and protect us throughout our journey.

When my children were born, I was determined that they would be brought up in a home filled with love and laughter and nurturing. And when the time came, they would have the FREEDOM to choose their path in life, and they would get all the support they would ask from us as their parents.

That is not to say they were feral, they made their choices, and with our experiences and guidance, they still made their own path in life. The life that we bring into this wonderful world of ours, needs nurturing and propping up until it is ready to have total freedom, just like a seedling growing in the garden.

It has broken my heart on many occasions when I've watched and listened to parents forcing their children into a direction that is not of their choosing. That child will struggle and feel tortured because their gut instinct is pulling them one way, but they are forced in another by parents who think they know best. Those souls then struggle with life, not fitting into that path.

I was born in Tunis North Africa at the beginning of the 50s. My mum was Italian and my dad Maltese. Ten months after my birth, my brother Louis was born. He was two months premature and had trouble from the day he was born. I was responsible for watching over him and would get shouted at or told off if he got up to no good.

Like sticking bread dough or buttons up his nose or anything else he could lay his hand on. Saying he was a challenge was an understatement. Yes, I started being responsible for my siblings from the age of two as I was in my photo on the cover of the book.

The one-bedroom flat my parents had rented when they got married was now too small, and we moved. Mum had two miscarriages after Louis was born, and five years after I was born, my brother Albert was born. There were now two brothers I was responsible for looking after.

My paternal Grandmother was Maltese and was born in the Governor's Palace in Malta along with her thirteen siblings. She fell in love and eloped to Tunis with her love a Maltese Catholic priest. They had three boys, and my dad was the youngest. My mum and dad met in their 40s as dad had been married before.

(When I was old enough about fourteen, my dad told me that he had married a prostitute, but because she could not have children, he left her. As he told me that, I began to cry and feel so terribly sad for his wife. He had treated her like a commodity. I firmly believe that my mum's family disowned her because of what my dad was like. She had no contact with them ever again. I honestly believe that was not of her choosing, and my dad's character had a lot to do with it).

Mum's maternal Grandmother's family originated from Sicily and had moved to Tunis many years previous, and her paternal grandparents were Italian. My mum had two siblings: a brother and a sister. The only one that stuck by my mum and never lost contact until Auntie's death was her mum's brother and his wife, who eventually moved to Antibes in the South of France. The languages that were spoken at home were

French and Italian if my parents did not want us to know what was being said.

Then whenever we got together with Nan and Uncles dad would talk to his mum in Maltese, my uncles would talk to all of us in French, or sometimes, Uncles would talk in Italian to Mum out of respect for her being Italian I suppose. Therefore, I grew up hearing and knowing many languages Arabic, Maltese and Italian words whilst speaking French.

Anyway, once again we had to move home as the flat was again too small for the five of us. The apartment we eventually moved to before coming to England was on the second floor and took one whole corner of the building. Mum loved plants, and Dad had wired up on the outside of the railings plant pots, and Mum had painted them all different colours. One half of the veranda/balcony was nearly always in the sun, and we had an awning where I was allowed to wind the leaver and bring shade and coolness on the tiled floor.

The height of the balcony wall was around four feet plus ten inches of railing. It was lovely and cold in the summer sitting on the tiled floor leaning against the wall and looking into the lounge. Mum would make us fresh lemonade and give us a glass straight from the fridge, hmmm.

There was a corner on the veranda where my dad had built us a large rabbit hutch high up enough for the rabbits to have fresh air. It was well sheltered and so ready to be occupied. Within a couple of days, my dad had brought home two rabbits: one white and the other white with black patches. Within a few weeks, the rabbits had babies, and Louis and I would climb on a stool and look through the meshing hoping to catch a glimpse of the babies.

We never got to see the babies as my dad had told us that because we were watching them all the time, they ate the babies. Cry well you never heard such a sad and guilt-ridden child. It had been my fault that those dear little rabbits had died. Louis on the other hand took it all in his stride.

Dear little Albert was too small to even know what was going on. Mum had shown him the rabbits, but he never showed any interest. After that, Dad took the rabbits back to the market where he had purchased them.

Right outside our flat when looking through the railings of the balcony, there were five roads all merging to a sort of roundabout. One day, I was sitting on the floor playing with my dolls and heard a terrible crash and a commotion, screaming and crying. I got up to look, and it was a lorry coming out of one road and had crashed into a person on a bicycle. I could hear someone shouting leaning over the rider of the bike it had been the lady's young son who was killed in the accident, and they had taken his body away, but one parent kept bending down and picking something up.

My mum had told me that they were collecting the child's teeth (I have no idea why my mum would want to tell me this at the age of seven; it was bad enough that I had witnessed the aftermath of the accident). That has been with me all my life, and every time I hear an ambulance or there has been an accident with a cyclist, that awful memory comes back to me.

On a lighter note but just as serious, Albert was beginning to walk and climb and getting into all sorts of mischief. His favourite game would be to stand on anything he had to hand and pick up a plant pot or one of his toys and lob them over the balcony down onto the road or pavement below. His books, toys, anything he fancied, and I then became the fetch and retrieve child.

In the hot summer evenings, we would have local traders coming round with their barrow lit with lanterns, and they would shout out what they were selling, either peanut brittle or almond brittle, roasted chestnuts and even little posies of Jasmine. Mum or Dad would sometimes go down when we'd stayed up late, and we would have some to eat; the smell from these barrows would drift right up to the balcony in the warm night air.

Looking from the balcony into the apartment, there were big doors into the lounge on both sides of the room. The dining table was large with a lovely polished top with eight chairs around it. On one of the walls, there was a huge framed picture of the Queen of England. Against the far wall was a large dark wood sideboard for Mum to store all the crockery cutlery and table linen.

Unfortunately, we had quite a lot of small lizards that would come in through the open doors and somehow managed to get into the sideboard, and it was Mum's fright at these creatures when she would open one of the drawers, and a lizard would jump out and scare her so much that she miscarried my baby brothers on two separate occasions. We were never told about this. (I only found out when going through paperwork many years later. Unfortunately, one baby she miscarried at six month's term, and the child was given a burial plot.)

I have heard it said many times that when you die as a baby or a child their soul carries on growing, so when it is my time to die I am looking forward to meeting my brothers and giving them lots of love and hugs (Oh, where's my hankie?),

When we reached school age, Louis and I were sent to a convent, and our school friends were of different nationalities, but everyone spoke French at school and also learnt Arabic. I suppose due to Mum's miscarriages, Mum and Dad decided Mum should have some home help for a few hours a day, just until we'd got a bit older. Apparently, quite a few ladies or young women were employed but never stayed very long. Many years later, I had found out that my dad was a womaniser and wonder if that had been the reason for them leaving.

Then one day, a lady called Zena applied and got the job. She was lovely, kind always smiling and chewing gum. She was dressed in traditional clothing with a headscarf tied at the back covering her hair. She wore gold earrings that dangled from her stretched thin earlobes. She had a very thin tanned face covered with loads of wrinkles.

When she smiled, she had brown teeth, and some were covered with gold. She told my mum that as a young ten year old, she was married off to a man very much older than her, but they never had children. So she was looking forward to being with us.

She would take us to school and bring us home. Sometimes going and getting a couple of bits in the souks for Mum before getting us from school. God forbid if anyone picked on us or wanted to hurt us, she looked after us like her own. When the floors in the flat needed washing down, she'd pick up the hem of her skirt on either side of her body and pull it into her waistband so as not to get it wet. She would sing Arabic songs and dance whilst doing her work and chewing gum of course.

On one occasion, I vividly remember we were still at school, and there was an almighty thunderstorm, and it had rained so much and so quick that the drains overflowed and the floodwater was knee-high for Zena. Rather than wait until the waters had subsided, she came to collect us from school, fearing that if we were late home, Mum would be worried sick. She carried Louis and me one on each hip holding us tight and reassuring us all the time.

As we got closer to home where the floodwaters had not come up that high, she put us down, and the bottom of her clothes were dripping. Mum thanked Zena and sent her home early to change and dry off.

My mum was very superstitious, and when a thunderstorm was approaching, she would rush round to put out on the window sills a special kind of bread roll that people would buy in the grocer for protection from the lightning.

I'm afraid when it rained it did rain like a monsoon. Mum has had me hooked on some of her superstitions all my life. Never leave your cutlery crossed on the plate at the end of a meal. Don't put shoes or a hat on the bed or a table and thunderstorms still terrify me, although I did show some heroism when my children were young so that I did not pass on the fear to them. Well, you have to don't you? You can't give them your hang-ups.

I don't know where the superstition about the 'evil eye' came from though, but many nations know about it. Once a week, my mum and Zena would clean the flat right through, and as the floors were tiled, it was easy to just wash down everywhere. Afterwards, Mum would take some dried leaves put them in a dish and burn them, and she would walk around the apartment directing the plate into every corner to take away the evil eye and cleanse the air.

Also, once a month, Mum would take a dish, put water into it and a drop of oil in the centre and then would walk around into each room. People who were envious or wished you harm you could end up with a migraine headache or worse.

For stronger cures, my mum would call the landlady who knew more about this practice, and she would get a soup plate and pour water into it then adding the drop of oil in the centre. She would pass it over the head of the person suffering bad headaches whilst she muttered some words. Whatever she said always worked. The reference to the evil eye cure is also mentioned in great detail in the space clearing book by Karen Kingston.

I remember vividly the Jewish family who lived in the apartment below us. Every Friday before mealtimes, I was asked to go down to light the stove for the Mum to cook the evening meal because her religion forbade her to perform this task of lighting stoves on Fridays. Can you imagine asking a seven-year-old nowadays to light a gas stove with matches?

We did not have holidays only the odd time where all of us including Nan and Uncles would go to a restaurant by the sea and be there for a few hours.

My brothers and I did not play when we were out only if we visited the beach, which was not very often. I do not even remember celebrating a birthday until I was very much older and once we had moved to England.

A few years before we moved to England, my dad had rented a shop not far from home, and he sold watches, repaired them and also sold a very small amount of jewellery. He called the shop Greenwich (for Greenwich Meantime).

On some days, Dad would take me to work with him. I was with him to look after the front of the shop should anyone come in and take some of his stock from the glass cabinet. I learnt very early on to read people's faces, and if I thought someone was not quite right, I would call my dad out with the excuse that I had knocked something over. The shop was about twenty feet in length by around fifteen feet wide.

Two-thirds were in the front of the shop with a glass cabinet showing an array of watches and jewellery. The back was separated by a curtain so Dad could hear what was going on in the front. Unfortunately, the back of the cabinet did not have any glass and anyone coming in could lean over the counter and take some of Dad's stock. Basically, as a seven-year-old, I was to be the watchman for the day (sorry for the pun).

There were not many occasions where I had to call my dad when I had been wary of a particular customer(s). I was very apprehensive about doing this task for my dad, but I was also very scared if an item was taken when I was asked to watch over the merchandise. I knew that my dad would flip and everyone at home would suffer too.

Before we moved to England, Dad would teach us a couple of English songs—mostly Daisy, Daisy. So that we could blend in as quickly as possible; we should not mention where we came from but just say we were British (What? Was he having a laugh he really was being delusional? How could we hide our colour and the fact that we spoke French? This is where some children's hang-ups come from 'delusional parents').

England—Victoria

We all moved to England from North Africa in 1959, my mum and dad, my brothers and I together with my dad's mum and his two elder brothers who helped my parents financially for the trip.

Zena had begged Mum to take her with us, but my parents did not have the money for her fare. I cried so much at leaving her behind. We were only allowed one toy each and for my parents only the bare minimum of possessions.

I was a lonely child. My parents believed that girls should learn from a young age that their purpose in life was all about housework, cooking, cleaning and looking after the home and family, then marry, have babies and keep husband and family happy. My happiness was not important, and I grew up firmly believing all that rubbish all of my life until my husband passed away.

When we arrived in England, we went straight to a small flat in Victoria. My uncle Victor had visited England a few months before and secured the lodgings. Within a week or so, Louis and I were registered at the local school.

Being in a foreign country, eating different food and not fitting in at all were very traumatising for me as I was a very sensitive and quiet child. Trying to learn the language was hard enough, but trouble always found me because of my tanned skin and French accent. I'd never known bullying, and I could not understand what I was doing wrong and why the other children didn't like me. At home, I was always treading on eggshells as anything would set my dad off shouting, throwing things and even punching the furniture.

Looking back on his severe mood swings, I believe it was partly due to his leaving the business behind and needing to take on menial jobs in England in order to make ends meet.

Sometimes Uncle Victor would take us out for a walk around and visit St James's Park. We would walk through the concourse of Victoria Station, and he would see a chocolate vending machine. He would put some money in it, slide the metal bar and out came the chocolate—white and pure nectar. I have remembered that taste and smell all of my life and think of him so fondly when I see a Milky Bar.

Clapham South in London

We lived in Victoria for a few months until Uncle Victor found a house for us to rent in Clapham South London. We had the ground floor, and Uncles and Nan had the top floor. I think the landlord called the accommodation maisonettes. Once again Louis and I changed schools.

For the first couple of days, my mum took us to school; then we would come home by ourselves. Sometimes, the headmaster would take the class and ask each one of us, in turn, to come to his desk and go through our work. I was only nine at the time and was desperate to mix in and not be the odd one out.

Standing by Mr Gibson and listening to his comments, I suddenly felt his hand at the top of my leg, and I jumped. "You are doing very well at school," he told me and proceeded to put his hand on my bottom, but I didn't know why. I thought he was going to spank me like my dad did when he was angry, but he didn't. It wasn't until I was much older that the penny dropped, and I was horrified. I had never told my parents.

One day, I woke up to find that Mum wasn't home, and Dad had told us that she was not well and had to go to the hospital. Then a policeman came to see my dad and spoke on the doorstep. When he went, Dad was upset and told us that Mum had lost the baby she was carrying, but she would be home soon. There was no phone at home so I suppose that would have been the most appropriate way to let Dad know. I was very upset for Mum and my baby brother.

Just before my tenth birthday, the landlord who had also moved from North Africa came to the house and asked to speak to my dad and uncles. I heard shouting and an argument brewing; Mum was worried about what was being said. It turned out that the landlord was giving notice to my Nan and uncles because he had friends (an Italian family of five who were looking for accommodation). He wanted the top floor maisonette within the week and said if it was not vacated by Friday, he would come with men and torches and burn all our possessions. One way or the other, there would be trouble.

Friday came, and I had no idea what was happening until my dad explained to me what was going to happen and that he wanted me to take Mum, Louis and Albert and run up to the police station up the road and tell them what was happening. I was only nine for pity sake, how could he ask that of me. I was so panicked and scared that everyone would die in the house if I did not say the right thing.

When we got to the police station I blurted out the story to the officer behind the desk as best I could, he could see I was panicked and out of breath. He told me not to fret that someone would come along soon and not to worry.

We rushed back home; my heart was in my throat; my legs were like jelly; I could not go any faster; Louis was close behind me with Mum dragging Albert beside her. The landlord and the men were still outside the house threatening, and as I went up the path, I shouted to Dad the policeman said someone is coming soon. With that, the men fled, and the landlord said he would be back, and he went as well. Nobody ever came as I don't think the policeman believed our dilemma.

This landlord was a nasty piece of work. He owned quite a few properties and ruled the tenants with a rod of iron. I had once told him that I was being bullied at school for my colour, and he swore to me that if I drank loads of milk every day I would soon get rid of my tan. I did that for a very long time, but from then on, I could no longer take milk in anything, and having milk at school made me physically sick. To this day, I am still intolerant to milk and dairy.

Before finishing junior school, I was being bullied so much by three Greek sisters who would follow me home every day. One day, it had been so bad that I got home crying and not wanting to go back to school. When Mum found out the problem, she said that she would sort it. I couldn't understand how as her English was so bad.

To my utter horror, the following day, I was nearing home with the girls in tow, and as I turned the corner, there was my mum. I was so scared because I knew there was going to be trouble. As my mum met me, she grabbed my hand and turned me towards them and said, "You are going to slap one of them in the face. I don't care which, and if you don't, I will pull your knickers down in front of them and give you a good hiding."

I was dumbstruck. I didn't want to hurt the bullies. I just wanted them all to stop. As I got closer to them. Mum said in French, "go on hit her." Half-heartedly, I slapped her, and she stood there shocked and said she would tell her mum, but nothing ever happened.

Move to Streatham Hill

Within a week, my Nan and uncles found a ground floor maisonette in Streatham about three miles away. The new tenants moved in upstairs and were very rowdy and noisy, and my dad was not happy with the situation. Just before I was due to start secondary school, the top floor maisonette where Nan and Uncles lived became vacant, and we moved in too, all under one roof again.

Many of you will be horrified at my saying this to you, I had to share a bedroom with my two brothers all my growing up years until I got married at the age of nearly twenty-two. My dad did not believe that we should ask for Council housing as we were not born in England. At times, he would say not even God can make me change my mind. What God had to do with the situation I would never know.

The secondary school my parents had chosen for me was about three miles from home in Tooting Broadway and around thirty–forty minutes of bus journey. My parents in their infinite wisdom decided that at the age of eleven, I should go to a convent (no boys you see), so I could learn discipline and better my education for my future prospects (oh of course to get married and having babies, silly me).

That was a laugh and a half. You'll understand why later. Being bullied or being picked on never stopped, and it carried on all through my life. My brothers on the other hand went to a local secondary school and were home early enough to do their homework by the time I got home. They would have their dinner and be out with friends.

On Mondays, in my first year, we would have games, and we would travel by underground from school to Morden. Once we were finished and going home, we would all go our separate way. Mine was the underground to Balham then up to the British Rail line to Streatham Hill, no other stops but a longish journey between the stations. One day, I got into a single carriage (do you remember those?) and sat down by the door; I suddenly noticed an elderly chunky man at the other end on the opposite side to where I was sitting.

When I looked across and noticed him, he was exposing himself and fear struck in me you cannot imagine. There had been no time to change compartments as the train had started off the second I shut the door. I was praying that I would be alright and thankfully after what seemed a lifetime the platform edge came into view, and I was off like a shot not even looking behind me and running up the two long staircases like a bat out of hell.

I stood in the foyer panting like mad and shaking. I needed to calm down before making my way home which would take me about fifteen minutes to walk. Hopefully, I would get home before Dad.

Oh yes, the dreaded dinner time, always at around 6 pm God help you if you were not home. Mum would always dish up a soup, then the main meal followed by the dessert. Everything was homemade, and at times, dinner would take her all day especially if it was Pasta al Forno or Ricotta Ravioli. Even the pasta sauce was homemade, and at times, when she could not buy, any she would make her own ricotta (Yummy). The only meals I really hated were tripe and cauliflower soup. Yuk.

As we got older, the boys would sometimes want to do something or go somewhere, and Dad would not allow them, but Louis and Dad would have huge arguments, to the point where my dad would shove his plate across the table in anger so hard that all the glasses of water would topple over with water going into the meals, across the table and onto the carpeted floor. My mum would start to cry, and she and I would clear the table because, that night, we would not finish our meal.

Or on occasions, Dad would already come home in a mood goodness knows why, and he would start rowing with Mum, and it would spill onto dinner time, and by which time he was so angry, he would take it out on the furniture by punching holes in the backs of chairs or throw his dinner plate across the table. If he didn't like the meal that particular night, that too would go flying.

Very rarely was there a conversation at the dinner table. Mum and I would bring in the meal from the kitchen; the television would be on; and the only noise you heard was the cutlery on the plates. One thing though he would always thank Mum for a nice meal provided it had been to his liking that is.

In all of my school years, I could count on one hand how many girls I made friends with and tried to invite them home for a visit. My mum would always find something wrong with any friend I had the chance to invite home, and Mum would find a reason for me not to invite them again. I was not allowed to visit them at their home. My brothers were allowed anything like that. I was always the one to go for errands up the high street and set and clear the table at mealtimes.

As I never went anywhere special except for compulsory church on Sundays with my brothers, my best clothes were always in the wardrobe (one dress and a couple of skirts and tops), but as I got a bit older, Saturday mornings running errands for my mum were the best as I could wear something nice, providing it was not raining. My mum would send me with a shopping list, and the first stop would be the coffee shop in Streatham High Street, and I would ask for half a pound of 'medium ground continental' coffee and a packet of chicory.

Then on to the butchers, and these errands were the highlight of my week. I had freedom and no eggshells to walk on. I was me well sort of you know what I mean. I could take my time and window shop, and if I took too long, I blamed it on the queues in the shops.

One day, I walked into the butcher's shop and did a double-take, there behind the counter was my idol, Clint Eastwood, no silly me but a flipping good look-a-like though. On my way home, I'd thought, 'Oh my God, it will be even more brilliant going to the shops on Saturdays'. The butcher boy was well over six feet and really skinny, blond spiky hair, and he had a red face every time he had to speak to the customers. I was well and truly smitten; for the first time in my fifteen years, I was looking at boys and not film stars in my magazines.

At home, I only had the painted built-in wardrobe cupboard door behind my headboard to stick one or two pictures up, and then I got laughed at for doing so by my brothers, or they would draw a moustache or glasses on the pin-ups.

Before we started having holidays, Dad would book us on London Transport family outings. They were outings for the workers and their families on concessionary fairs going to the seaside on a red double-decker bus. Dad always got us to sit upstairs so that we had a good view of the surrounding areas. On one of these trips, Mum and Dad were sitting in front, Louis and Albert behind them and I was behind them sitting on the aisle seat.

As we were going along, I could see the bridge ahead and instinctively knew we would not get under, at the point of impact I leant forward with my face hugging my knees. This saved me from severe facial injuries because the upright bar in front of me was sheared off along with most of the roof, which had concertinaed at the back of the bus.

We all got ushered off the bus and into the pub up the road for a cup of tea whilst they organised another bus to take those of us still wanting to make the trip. Dad did not want the pub for us so we stayed outside. A few of the people sitting right at the back of the bus had to go to the hospital with minor injuries, and a while later, another bus was brought down.

Many had decided that we should carry on with the trip. Dad could not believe that I had not been hurt and thanked God for my actions. He kept asking me how was it I had known what to do, and I kept telling him that someone had made me do it.

When I was about thirteen, we started having holidays in a caravan in Hastings. Dad had watch repairing jobs from some of his workmates, and the small earnings from that gave us the chance to have a holiday once a year. I am finding it difficult to describe the tension felt by all of us. We would be in the same place as our dad for the whole week.

That alone set our teeth on edge. I was going to have to walk on eggshells all the time. My dad was the only happy one. He was on holiday, and we should all be happy and smiling and enjoy ourselves as he would be spending a lot of money in order to give us this holiday.

My brothers and I were not allowed to wander off on our own; we had to stay together. On the odd chance that we did go to the pier, my parents sat outside; Louis would wander off whilst I stayed with Albert. The few holidays we all had together had been full of rows, and Dad would get angry at anything and anyone, but on the occasions that he was happy and laughing, we would look at each other and say, "Who is this person?"

My dad was a womaniser, but God helps anyone who looked at my mum or made any innocent approaches towards her, he was like a man possessed. He would tell us what meals were best to eat, and then we'd get picked on for not finishing a meal, oh and it went on and on.

The last two holidays we all had together was on the Isle of Wight renting a couple of rooms just up the road from the pier at Ventnor.

I vividly recollect that the age of fifteen was one of the most challenging and demoralising hurtful years in my life. One that 'God forgive me' I'd wished my dad was dead. What an awful thing to admit. I'd been working hard to learn English and trying to put up with all the horrid bullying and harrowing times at home, the bullying was still going on at school too, and I was to experience another humiliating change in my life.

It was the end of the fourth year, and the reports came out as usual in sealed brown envelopes, I dreaded it as I was always sixteenth or lower down in my grades out of thirty-two. Personally, only having lived in England for the last seven years at the time and having to learn English, I thought I had achieved quite a lot in those few years and had done better than some of my English schoolmates. The Reverend Mother and my dad did not see it that way, and for me to achieve any good grades on leaving secondary school, I had no option but to repeat the fourth year add this in (with all my classmates leaving to move on). Horrified and humiliated and what seemed to me being punished for having worked so damned hard, they hadn't even consulted me as to what my opinion was or anything.

I could not believe it; I had worked so hard much more than my brothers; I'd stayed home all the time keeping my parents happy by doing everything they asked of me. My new fourth year classmates were more snobbish than the previous. I had to put up to more bullying and teasing and being picked on and humiliatingly last in being chosen for team events. There was a girl at school who lived very carefree and nothing fazed her, not even being threatened with expulsion. She could not understand why my life at home was the way it was.

One afternoon, she decided to bunk off school and go home, and she invited me to go with her. I told the Nun taking the next lesson that I felt poorly and was going home. My stomach was all knotted up at having told a lie. I went with my new school friend, she had her own front door key, wore a leather jacket, smoked, had a boyfriend, and her parents were ok with it all. To them, I must have stood out like a boil on someone's nose. We lived two completely different lives.

It was great bunking off because there was no bullying; I was too far from home to be seen by my parents, but although I liked the freedom, I knew it was wrong and that there would be consequences. I suppose in a way it was my way of expressing anger at how I was being treated, and I wanted to get one upon them.

The skies fell in on me when my friend and I decided we would take a couple of days off school. The Reverend Mother wrote to my parents asking if there was a problem with me as she had not seen me at school for a couple of days; she knew dam well what was going on as both my friend and I had been seen together by classmates.

When my dad came home from work, I could hear raised voices in the lounge between him and Mum; I was doing my homework in the bedroom. Dad came in and told me to go into the lounge in such a manner that I knew I was in for a humongous clash with him. He asked me all the usual questions of where had I been, what had I been up to and who was this girl.

Now, my dad was very good at asking questions but always disbelieved your answers no matter what the situation, He was always right, and according to Dad, we always told lies. So all the truthful explanations, I gave in order to make things not so bad for myself was to no avail, he grabbed my arm and muttered something to my mum at the same time as he yanked me down onto his knees, I was struggling to get away as he proceeded to pull my pants down and gave me a thrashing.

I could not believe what had just happened, I was in floods of tears with the pain, the humiliation and embarrassment. To make matters worse, my brothers were laughing because they said I was stupid for telling the truth; I should have lied like they always did.

My friend was expelled from school as she was always away from school and making trouble with the teachers. I got on with my schoolwork and still got picked on. Louis had also started to pick on me, and we would have huge arguments.

Mum would get so fed up with us arguing and rowing that she would shout at us to stop and when we didn't she would throw wooden spoons at us from the kitchen. This spoon throwing went on for a long time but only when Dad was not home because if we rowed when Dad was home God help us.

I had no choice in doing as I was told to do by my mum or dad but not by Louis. On one occasion I chased him along the landing from the bedroom where he had been constantly picking on me whilst I was doing my homework, and he got to the bathroom and shut the door behind him and locked the door. I stood there banging on the wooden panel between the two panes of glass on either side when suddenly this searing pain came to my arm. Blood everywhere, I had missed the wooden panel and put my wrist through the thickened glass on one side.

My uncle Victor was called up, he called a taxi and whilst waiting made a tourniquet at the top of my arm to reduce the bleeding. Bless him he did his best, but by the time, it took Mum and me to get to the hospital in Tooting, my arm was going blue and the doctor was not happy. I had eight stitches in my wrist (right hand of course) so that meant I could not do any writing for a couple of days—but I still had to go to school the following day.

At the end of that year, my grades were better, and I had the chance to move up to the fifth form and perhaps even onto the sixth form. At the end of the fifth form, I managed to get six CSE passes something my brothers did not achieve. I was so keen to go on to further education as I wanted to be a teacher, and for the first time, I felt a sense of achievement. Having said that, my dad did not think so as the school report still said, 'could do better'. So in his eyes, I still was not trying hard enough.

Discussion time with my parents came when I had to decide my future and it was quite exciting, choosing something for myself. I told my parents that I wanted to stay at school or go to college and become a teacher. Their faces dropped, and they looked at each other, 'a teacher' my dad angrily said, his face full of horror and red with anger 'what for' he replied questioning my intelligent choice. You don't need to be a teacher you will get married and look after your husband and children and keep everyone happy.

I could not believe it; in the space of a year, I was suffering yet another blow to my future plans and aspirations. Looking back on this scenario it reminds me of the film The Big Fat Greek Wedding. The Dad in the film reminded me so much of mine. Eventually, I persuaded my parents to allow me to go onto sixth form and learn typing and commerce and improve my English Language subjects, but they said I should forget about being a teacher.

What the hell was I going to be when I left at eighteen? Where was I going to find a 'husband' as they wanted me to? Or had they already got someone in mind? Please God no.

By the time I had left school, I had never had a birthday party or gathering with friends, also never been allowed to go to a party, dance or show let alone a pub. My classmates would invite me to join them to see the Walker Brothers or such groups. I would never even ask Mum and Dad as I knew it would create more sermons and anger from Dad.

School trips I did attempt to ask about, but I was given all sorts of excuses, so like everything else I missed out on them too. Oh yes, and I remember on hundreds of occasions my brothers, or I would ask about Mum's family, and we would always get fobbed off. If Dad was around, and he'd hear us asking he would go off on one.

You never dared to ask him, but my grandmother told me once where she had been born and that her mother had been a maid and her dad a footman. We never knew anything else.

My First Job

At the age of sixteen, I got myself a Saturday job at our hairdressers and liked it as it gave me time away from home. Dad had stopped my pocket money of two and six because I was earning my own money.

Then at the age of seventeen, I got a job working for Derry and Toms department store in High Street Kensington. I first worked in the gift department then on the cigarette kiosk. Louis after a while decided he would work there too and started in maintenance then on the customer lifts and eventually in the giftware department. We would never travel to and from work together he said that I would frighten the girls away as they would think I was his girlfriend.

My dad had been talking to people at work (London Transport now called Transport for London) and managed to find me a job in the cheque clearing department. He firmly believed being a girl that this was all I was capable of doing once leaving school. I had not been consulted or asked if I wanted to work for the company.

All the exams I had passed were for nothing. I was paper shuffling and the salary was £11 per week with free travel on the buses and underground. What was the point, I was not allowed out and did not go anywhere and Louis did not want me to go out with him as he said I would cramp his style.

I hated the job Dad had found me and it made me depressed and ill to the point that I was heading for a nervous breakdown. Something inside told me that if I did not get out I would be ill forever. I questioned myself thinking, what was all my hard work at school for, what had I gained all that knowledge for?

One lunchtime, I went to a temping agency called Alfred Marks and registered for office work. I was given a typing exam and was asked various questions about my background and where I worked. I was offered £26.00 per week and more if I worked extra hours, or used different machines on my assignments. I went home elated and determined that I was going to get my own way.

When I told my dad I was leaving London Transport and explained about the job I was going to do, he admitted that I had done something good, and he apologised for sending me to a place that was not suitable for me. A first for me as my dad always proclaimed he was never wrong. This one would have to go down in history.

My first temping job was in Victoria and it lasted eleven weeks as the company Manager was very happy with me. After that, I got further assignments and was asked to go permanent with several, but I did not want to get tied down to one place or get involved in office politics. One day, I was walking towards Victoria Station going home and this man approached me and said that he could get me a job in a Peter Cushing movie and if I was interested to join him and others at the coffee shop around the corner.

I have no idea why I said it, but I told him that I was meeting my dad, and I would need to let him know first. I don't think I finished my reply, and he was gone. We all know what he had in mind. Not me though not until I was talking to one of my work friends much later.

I then got a job for a debt collecting agency in Lee Green, and I met my first boyfriend, I was nineteen, and he was a year younger. I was elated at the thought that he loved me, something I had not had before. My parents never showed their love for me or ever said 'I love you'. There was no love at home just respect for each other as parent and child.

Things were going so well that we got engaged. We would go up to London and frequent pubs and meet his friends. He had by then also changed jobs and was a window dresser for the Army and Navy department store in Victoria High Street.

His attitude towards me started to change. When we were out he would suggest a place to visit and if I didn't agree he would punch or kick me. In the street in front of the public, he didn't care, afterwards, he would apologise and say I had just made him angry. It was always my fault as it had been all my life with my dad.

On one occasion my parents and Albert were going away to the Isle of Wight for a week self-catering and asked if we wanted to join them. My parents were offering to pay for both of us. He was all smiles and happy. It wasn't long before he started all over again. He would want to go somewhere, and I didn't so he sneaked in a punch.

This went on through the week and then one day we were on the beach which he had agreed to, and we ran into the sea waist high, and he was pushing me about and then started to hold my head under water. Struggling and pushing him away

I'd come back up, and he did this a few more times where I then struggled to breathe as I came back up. To my parents watching us, they would have thought we were larking about. That was the last time I went near the water.

The final time he abused me, was when we had been going to Bayswater to a pub, and we were crossing the road when he started to kick me because he wanted me to pay for the evening as he had no money after buying his cigarettes for the week. He kept catching up with me and kicking me with his Doc Martin boots and then punching me, people were staring, and I was shouting and crying for him to stop. Again he apologised, and we went into the pub. My legs were throbbing that evening.

I was now getting really scared because I thought he would one day kill me if I didn't change things. That following night I made an excuse and asked his mum if I could go round as I knew he would not be home that evening. I explained to her what had been going on and that I could not be with him anymore. I gave her the ring to give back to him and went home. Getting home I was so distraught, hurt and ashamed I was determined my parents would never find out the real reason.

All my life I have been extremely good at hiding any trauma or abuse I suffered. I could not bear people knowing how stupid and naive I had been and that it had probably been my fault in the first place. When I got home that night, I was really upset and was crying and told my parents that it was over as we had too many differences of opinion.

The real reason was that I had lost the feeling of being loved by him if you could call it that. I have not given him a name in telling you the story because he traumatised me so much. He had been my first experience in real-life with a young man, and I had managed to get away before being seriously hurt or killed.

Whilst temping for an Architects firm in Grosvenor Square, I was asked to join the company for a permanent position. I had been temping for them a number of months and the accountant was loathed to carry on paying the high fees to the agency. We worked out a suitable salary, and I joined them permanently. The boys in the offices were really great and fun to work with, they were all different ages, and I got on with all of them.

My job was to carry on as typist to the site team, but later on, I became PA to one of the two Directors and although it sounded daunting the job was great, a mixture of copy typing, dictating machine and all the other office jobs. The boys in the offices had found out about my engagement break up and gave me great support and had told me that I was better off without him. I did get offers of dates from some of them, but I declined as I was still very nervous about any relationship.

One lunchtime, they asked if I would go to the pub with them for lunch, I was not too happy as the CEO was due that afternoon to give us all a pep talk, but they would not take no for an answer. We all walked to the pub, my first time in a pub on my own.

Six of the boys from the office came and a couple of the girls were supposed to come, but I later found out that it was not true and it was their way of getting me to the pub. They were trying to get me to get over my break-up, so they said.

The strongest drink I had ever had thus far was a light ale shandy, but they offered me a barley wine saying it was just a different company making the shandy. Having the pub lunch, laughing and joking I did not realise that they had given me another glass of the barley wine.

Time was nearing for the CEO's visit, and we had to clear one of the offices to accommodate all the staff being in one room for the meeting. I walked out of the doors and it was like I had been blown back by a really strong gust of wind. Everyone was playing down my reaction and said come on you can walk it off as one took me by the arm, I do remember them giggling a lot.

As we got into the office one of the boys said look take a drink of this homemade beer, beer settles the head and stomach. Unfortunately, for them, it made me even worse, and I ended up lying on the seating in reception crying my eyes out and wanting my mum.

They were panicking by now because the CEO was due soon; the doors opened, and Ivy the tea lady took one look at me and screamed at them, "What have you done to her? Look at her she is in a real state. What have they done to you my darling?"

I tried to tell her; then they divulged the horrible trick that they had played on me. Basically, they just wanted to see what I would be like drunk and nothing to do with the break-up. Dah!

The CEO's visit was nerve-racking for the boys as I was making unwanted comments during his speech whilst sitting on the edge of one of the tables swinging my feet back and forth saying that it was all boring, and I wanted to go home to bed. They were all really scared that I would get the sack and the joke would backfire on them.

Once the CEO had gone the boys could see the error of their ways and for my own safety too, they decided to drive me home. They were all aware of what my dad was like and that he would be home by the time they got me home. Like a bunch of scaredy-cat, two of them got me out of the car, and I stumbled to the front gate where they propped me up and turned to go, but I just stood there. One brave soul took me by the arm and helped me up the front step to the front door, rang the bell and was off.

By the time I turned to say 'bye all', I was talking to myself and facing the wrath of my mum. She told me to go to bed and not to be seen by my dad as the Mother of all rows and fights would take place. My dad always said that women of ill repute frequented pubs or women that were looking for trouble.

The boys always tried to fool me with jokes they would play on me. I remember one embarrassing time. I was typing up snagging lists for one of the chaps called Colin. He had been round one of the sites and had gone round recording his findings, but at one point, I could hear running water, and I could not hear the notes being dictated.

I went down to him in the general office and questioned the piece on the recording whilst playing it back to him. He turned laughing and said, "Oh sorry darling, I was having a pee at the time."

I was so embarrassed I didn't know what to say. I just said, "Oh really?" and made my way back to my office. Later, he came and apologised but had found it funny at the time.

The situation at home between Dad and Louis was getting worse and Louis was retaliating to Dad's restrictions. It was all the male hormones getting in the way. Louis decided that as he was now eighteen he could move out and get a flat as Dad would always include in his arguments with him, "While you are living in this house, you will do what I say." Louis left home and moved to Beckenham a few stops down the railway line.

Neither Louis nor my parents would give in and visit one another so (yes, you guessed it, I was made to visit Louis to make sure he was eating well, tidy his flat and help with the washing). I thought great I get all the grubby jobs again. He confided that he was having a good time and going out, and he had met a young woman and at one point he thought she may be pregnant. I was embarrassed and felt uncomfortable because Louis, and I had never spoken about that sort of thing.

Looking back I suppose it was due to the strict and Victorian attitude my parents had towards our upbringing. I was not happy at visiting him every fortnight, he was not my responsibility and to boot, Louis would ask me to keep his lifestyle secret from Mum and Dad and when I'd get home Mum and Dad would ask for all the details and I had to keep things from them, I hated being stuck in the middle.

Then one day Mum says she wanted to come with me when I next visited Louis. Dad apparently had stopped her from visiting Louis, but she could see Louis was not going to come home, and she wanted to see him, she missed her son and wanted to help in any way. So, on my next visit Mum came and was shocked at the area Louis was living in and how dingy his flat was. It was an ok visit and after that Mum took over visiting Louis. Dad did eventually go with her but only once.

At that office where I worked there was a young man called Trevor three years my senior who worked in another sector of the company on the top floor. Trevor had asked me out a couple of times, but I declined as I was nervous.

Remember I had not had friends up until the last chap. The experiences of boys so far had been, shall we say scary? And my brothers Louis in particular were no better.

Whilst Trevor was getting more keen on me my parents decided in their infinite wisdom that I should go and visit my mum's aunt and uncle in Antibes in the South of France to help me get over the breakup of my engagement. The arrangements were made, and I was off; I could not believe my luck, going on my own to stay with relatives I could only remember from photos and what they looked like but who were by now very elderly.

I was to live with them for two weeks. I landed at Niece Airport and was met by my aunt and uncle (I will call them that to make it easier). I recognised them from the photos and them with mine.

We arrived at their ground floor maisonette had something to eat and got ready for bed. I had waist-length jet black hair then and wondered how I could wash my hair and dry it when the time came. Everything they had was very basic but one, a bidet (well I had never seen one before and could not work out for quite some time what it was for).

Just as we were going to bed a knock came at the front door, the sound was so loud and seemed to boom through the flat that we all jumped. My uncle went to the door and it was a Gendarme, the police had been contacted by my parents because they had not received a call from me saying all was ok. My uncle reassured the Gendarme and told him that I would ring my parents in the morning.

There was no telephone at the flat and when I went to make a call home they both took me to the post office, and I had to request a connection to my parents' number, then I was asked to go to booth seven and I spoke to my parents. My dad was angry that I had put them through the scare, but he was glad I was ok. I handed the phone to Auntie who spoke with my mum it was the first time they had spoken to each other in twelve years.

Although Mum was limited in what she could say because of the way Dad was, she enjoyed the freedom of the phone call. Dad would write to them for Mum because Mum was not good at things like that, or so Dad would have us believe.

Only because my dad made sure she would always be beholding to him and it was his way of keeping a check on whatever Mum did and said. He stopped Mum from learning English from day one and made her look stupid if she attempted any words. My brothers did not help as they sided with Dad and made fun of her attempts.

Antibes South of France

The two weeks in Antibes were so strange for me because they reminded me so much of the kind of life we had left back home in Tunis. Everything was basic, no luxuries the buildings the language and uppermost, the way my aunt and uncle would suddenly invite themselves at their grown-up children's homes without notice.

They had three grown-up children and twelve grandchildren. I was a couple of years older than their eldest Grandson. We went to different places and also visited the outskirts of Marseille.

My aunt and uncle were the only family contact Mum had since marrying my dad. For reasons best known to them Mum was disowned by her entire family once she married, one cousin tried to see her from time to time then my dad found out and threatened him and that was that.

My auntie suffered from fits because of childbirth difficulties and none of us knew until she had one when I was there. Uncle quickly rushed to her and made her comfortable and ushered me out of the flat for a little while. It shook me to the core as I had never witnessed anything like it.

Apparently, once she was awake she could not remember having had a fit so I was told not to mention it. This was always at the back of my mind wondering when her next one would be.

Uncle had throat cancer many years previous and would only talk in a croaking manner. For the first couple of days, I found it upsetting not to be able to understand him as he tried so hard to take part in the conversations I was having with Auntie. All my mum knew about him was that he had an operation and it went wrong and that is how he'd ended up.

So when I eventually got home I not only told her the truth about Uncle but also that Auntie had told me that my mum's brother had moved from Tunis to Naples and had opened up a barber's shop and was married and had five children. My mum's sister and my grandmother had also moved from Tunis and were living on the France/Spain border. They were all relatives I would have relished to meet and be in contact with, but it was not to be.

When I came back from France my relationship with Trevor got serious, and we got engaged a few months later. We had decided to get engaged whilst my parents were on holiday, just the two of us, no fuss. We then told his parents who were happy or so I thought. When my parents got home we told them, and they were stunned, shocked, hurt and annoyed.

I don't think I can find any other negative words to describe their reaction. They did come round after a few days, but I didn't care, they had spoilt my happiness once again and made me feel that I had done something wrong again. They would not believe me when I said that there had been no celebration, party or even get together in their absence.

Eventually, Trevor's parents invited mine to their home for a little celebration and to meet. That was the start of a lot of my troubles for the next thirty-five years. I cannot believe how naive I was at only seeing the good in people. My upbringing had tattooed in my mind to have respect for your elders (in-laws in this case) and that they knew best. I was soon to be my husband's possession and his parents' too as my mum had been, and she still was to my dad.

The journey from London to West Malling in Kent near where Trevor and his family lived was quite long and gave Dad enough time to get worked up about the men in the family we were meeting. Would they get close to Mum, what would Dad do, he had to stop anyone from making advances.

By the time we got off the train, he was at boiling point, and Trevor's dad Terry pushed Dad to the brink when he first shook hands with Dad and promptly turned to Mum and kissed her on the cheek. Horror struck my heart as though the world had stopped for a couple of seconds, I looked at my dad his smile menacing ('Oh please God in heaven help us').

Trevor had two siblings a younger sister Lynda and an elder brother Luke. His dad Terry was a salesman for a giftware company and was at times away from home and before that he was a Royal Marine in the Second World War. Jean his mum worked part-time as a cleaner. Lynda was pregnant with her second child, and they had a boy called Ben. They all lived on a farm in a tied cottage where her husband Jeff worked.

Everyone was polite and tactful with a large helping of smiles. Trevor's mum was on tenterhook because she wanted to make a good impression and felt awkward at not being able to have a proper conversation with my mum whilst Trevor's sister Lynda thought everything was just a big joke.

After a few hours, we were being driven back to the station where the same thing happened again, handshake with Dad and a kiss on the cheek for Mum, and we said goodbye. The train journey home was just awful, Dad blaming Mum for enjoying the kisses given to her by Terry and Dad was threatening to do all sorts of things to him when they ever met again.

As we worked in the same building, Trevor and I saw each other every day. One day he asked me if I wanted to go down to Kent for the weekend, we would travel down together on Friday night after work and back up to work on Monday.

Wow, I thought, away from home on my own, and they weren't relatives yet. I had to get permission from my parents, and they agreed, but I needed to ring them when we got to Trevor's home and when I arrived back at work on Monday, oh yes, I was twenty-one by then and still having to do as I was told. Easy-peasy I thought if that's all I have to do that's brilliant.

I slept in Trevor's bed, and he took the settee in the lounge. In the morning he brought me in a mug of tea. I woke up with a terrible headache, something I was not use to. I presumed that it was the central heating, the different air from London, the nerves of being away for only the second time in my life.

I had a couple of painkillers but never really cleared it properly and the following day was the same. I stood on ceremony with everyone as I just could not relax and feel at ease. I was not use to being in mixed company let alone in-laws. Monday morning, we travelled to London to work, and I felt really good.

My headaches came and went as and when I was in Kent over the weekends. It got to the stage that I was no longer looking forward to those weekends. I felt on show all the time, Trevor's sister would pick on her husband and have arguments with him because he was giving me compliments. His brother Luke was the same with his compliments, and I would get uncomfortable in front of the women in the family.

We decided to set a date for the wedding for the following spring of 1973 but a couple of months after setting the date, in September 1972 my Nan became very ill and was ebbing away in a coma. She had been diagnosed with Leukaemia, and I offered to sit up and watch over her through the night whilst my uncles slept. I was quite happy to do it and it gave me the chance to be with her on my own as I listened to her mumbling and having what seemed like a conversation with my granddad.

I had never met him as he had passed away a number of years before I was born. She was the last of her generation that I would ever know and that saddened me and it made me think of my mum's parents. Relatives I would never get to know about or ever meet.

At 6:00 am, the following morning my uncle Victor came in and thanked me for giving him the chance to sleep and re-charge his batteries for his full day of caring. My other Uncle, Uncle Charles was no good at anything to do with running the home. I am sure he was born with a pen and paper in his hands and an adding machine by his crib. That is all he was doing every day of his life.

At 8:00 am, I was washed and dressed and out of the door to work. Halfway through the morning I got a phone call from home telling me that my Nan had passed away. It upset me greatly, but I could not show it too much when I got home because there was a lot of animosity between Nan and Uncles towards my mum.

My mum being home alone all day bothered me for some reason, I suppose it was because I was gradually doing more things away from home I felt sad for her with no female company, so I started calling her at lunchtimes from work and telling her what jokes the blokes at work had played on each other or me. She would tell me what was for dinner and if she had gone out to the shops.

I did this right up until I got married, and she would look forward to our conversation, conversations my dad could not get involved in or interfere in. It was our first time together at just being ourselves.

The wedding planning did not go smoothly, my dad was complaining that there were far more family members on Trevor's side than ours and it was a sit-down meal, which cost quite a lot of money. I bent over backwards trying to choose things that were really cheap.

Mum and I went up to Oxford Street to get my wedding dress, and I found one in the first shop we went in. It was much cheaper than Mum expected, and I knew that would please Dad. I think it was the third dress I had tried on and it was unanimous with everyone including Mum that this was the dress. It was an Aline dress with loads of lace and lace sleeves and a round neckline.

Mum took the dress home, and I was on the train down to Kent once again. Headaches were still in abundance and the penny still had not dropped. Do you remember what I told you about the evil eye?

Now I knew that my wedding day would not go well because of what my dad was like, basically like a time bomb ticking away. I was nervous because my dad had asked me to tell Trevor that my dad did not want his dad on the day to go near my mum, I had to tell Trevor because as time went on my dad was getting more and more agitated.

There were so many rows at home, mealtimes were horrendous. The response from Trevor's dad was just a load of laughter. He was egging my dad on, how could he? They were both going to ruin my day.

While the wedding arrangements were going along, Trevor wanted us to look for somewhere to live and Trevor's mum suggested we look at a house that was up for sale just along the road from them (I can hear some of you muttering under your breath). Yes, well with hindsight many of us would not have done many things in our lives). My family had always rented, and buying to me seemed such a daunting and scary commitment. We looked at the two-bed semi, and it had a large wood conservatory at the back.

We liked the property but needed to find the deposit. Mum and Dad stopped taking money off me to help us save, but Trevor's parents were not that generous. Eventually, we got the deposit and purchased the house with a mortgage. This did not go down well with his sister who was renting and did not live just up the road from her parents. She was so envious.

She would fake being unwell so that Trevor would go and see her. She faked falling down on the drive at her parents whilst pregnant with her second child in order to get attention. She made sure that the extended family was aware that I was not good for her brother and my mother-in-law was adamant that I had taken her son away.

(That is what I call my jumping from the frying pan (home) into the fire (married life)). At Christmas gatherings, they were all so hurtful as everyone including Aunts, Uncles, Cousins everyone would make me feel such an outsider to the point that I felt sick inside. They would be all over Trevor like a rash and pull him away to greet other members of the family and would always remind him of happy old times.

I never thought people could act so hurtful, just like bullies really. We only ever went to another Christmas gathering and it was in the year that Steven was born and that was just as bad, but at least I had Steven to cuddle and feed which took some of their attention away from me.

As I had no friends to speak of my Maid of Honour was my brother Louis' girlfriend. The day came, and eventually, my mum and brothers along with my Maid of Honour went in the car to the church. My dad and I were waiting for our car to arrive, and Dad turned to me and said, "if Trevor's dad goes anywhere near your mum and tries to kiss her he is going to get it," and he tapped his jacket pocket.

I looked and said, "What do you mean?" whilst mimicking his action.

Dad replied, "I have a knife in my pocket, and I shall have him."

Oh dear God in heaven, I was stiff with fear wishing I could call it all off. I was feeling sick and could not think of anything but his last words. Dad had a determined angry and fierce look on his face. Again he was ruining another of my special days.

I had no idea if Mum knew, I doubt it. We arrived at the church, and I was feeling as though I was going to the gallows rather than my wedding. Going down the aisle I was praying to everyone I could think of, for divine intervention, goodness knows what my face looked like. The ceremony over, and we went out to the back of the church for photos and then we all made our way to the hotel for the reception.

My heart was pounding so hard I thought everyone would be able to hear it, I was too scared to tell Trevor for fear he may tell his dad and it would escalate the situation. As we gathered for drinks at the reception Terry came over and kissed me on the cheek and then he kissed my mum too, as he did so I gazed over to Trevor's mum and sister, and they were both laughing.

They both knew how angry it made my dad, and they knew Terry had got one over on my dad. Nobody was stabbed, but it told me too how my in-laws were not bothered about ruining my big day and hadn't cared about any of our feelings.

Our First Home—Larkfield Kent

I remember this gift from my parents as though it was yesterday, on the eve of my wedding day Mum presented me with a box, her and Dad had bought for me for the wedding night. I was so embarrassed because of the implications this garment had. When I opened the box I was mortified it was a deep purple nylon negligee and see-through.

What? I was like a lamb to the slaughter, what were they thinking of, this would give Trevor the wrong impression of me. As with many women of my generation, the men enjoyed the night far more than their spouse, end of the story.

After a couple of weeks, on I felt trapped miles away from home with nobody to talk to and let off steam. Trevor would want us to visit his parents nearly every day of our honeymoon. If I mentioned anything about being unhappy at not having any time on our own Trevor would say I was imagining things. My parents would not hear of any words against Trevor, he was the apple of their eye; they loved him to bits, and he could do no wrong.

I had no friends as those I would eventually get to know were already good friends of my in-laws. My life was seriously beginning to resemble the life my Gran and mum had lived all their lives, both had lived isolated from friends and neighbours and families, and I was going down that same road.

When we got married we had a king-size bed from Trevor's parents, wardrobes donated by his cousins from Essex. Two wicker armchairs were also donated, a coffee table and a thick carpet in the lounge donated by his aunt near Brighton. No television and no telephone. My parents had bought us a Fridge. We had money left over from the purchase and bought a double oven cooker.

Within a couple of months of being married, I was at work and feeling unwell. I'd been sent to the medical office and explained my state of health to the nurse and asked for a couple of aspirin. She asked me a load of questions and turned to me and said, "I don't think they will do any good; you need to see your doctor. I believe you are pregnant."

"How did that happen?" I asked. How embarrassing and how stupid I must have looked.

Sure enough, I was pregnant, much to the horror of my husband who was not ready for fatherhood. Oh, and I was ready for motherhood was I? I had not been told by anyone about the facts of life. My mother would not have me mention periods or anything like that, and I never got a bra until I was a 34B and thirteen years old, my dad even chose to get involved with that episode in my life. How embarrassing? At school, the girls would laugh at me especially at games.

My parents were thrilled, my in-laws were pleased. Terry looked at me and said, "You enjoyed getting your house ready before the wedding I see," and winked at me. He was implying that Trevor had got me pregnant before our Wedding day whilst decorating our home before the wedding.

I quickly replied, "No that's not true," as I felt myself go red with embarrassment.

Walking away I recalled when Terry had once told me that I was sitting on a gold mine. I had no idea what he'd meant and it puzzled me for a very long time until I eventually asked Trevor. I was horrified and so embarrassed at his comment as at the time, I seemed to be the only one not knowing what he'd meant.

I worked until I was eight months pregnant and then I was home alone. Everyone was working and with Trevor still working in London he was gone all day from 6:00 am until 7:00 pm. My antenatal appointments were nerve-racking as I was always on my own.

No friends or neighbours to ask for moral support. All the neighbours knew my sister-in-law and what a drama queen and attention seeker she was. They got on with the parents but had no time for her.

I had always been on my own so that wasn't too much of a problem it was just in case I was given some bad news or something else. Being your first child so many things go through your mind, and I could not talk to my mum and ask things because we did not speak about that side of things, and I would have had to explain to my dad why I wanted to speak to Mum. There was no point asking Trevor's mum as his Sister would have made me look so stupid.

It was bad enough that she'd had a good laugh at me when she found out how naive I was about being pregnant. Even if I had a question on the days I rang Mum and Dad, I would have to ask my dad to relay the information because he would always hog the phone calls and tell me Mum was fine and said hello.

On the rare times that I did travel up to London to see them while I was pregnant, I found it difficult to talk to Mum. I would go into the kitchen and sit on the stall while she was preparing the meal, but within minutes, my dad would shout out from the lounge what are you talking about in there, where is everyone? He knew full well where we were but could not abide being left out and worried that we may be talking about him. He was like that all the time it was the same when I had been living at home.

I remember vividly, on one of my early phone calls home, not long after getting married my mum picked up, and I heard her voice, it was so nice. Dad had been in the loo, and she quickly said, "Do you think I could come and live with you?"

"There is no room Mum," by the time I had said that Dad had come back and taken the phone off Mum without giving me the chance to say cheerio. Walking back home from the phone box, I felt sick inside wondering why she would say that, but I had no way of finding out and the subject was never brought up again. I did make sure however that my visits to them were more regular even though it was such a drain on me.

I would have to get to West Malling Station by walking through the cow field. The long journey into Central London then another train to Streatham Hill Station and then the fifteen-minute walk to Mum and Dad's.

About a year after the wedding, my dad was pensioned off early due to ill health, and I thought at the time that he may have fixed it that way because he could not bear to think of Mum being home on her own with his two brothers living downstairs now they were both pensioners too. With Dad now home for good, he had started to tell Mum how to reorganise her way of doing things around the house, then the shopping and so on. Mum would not have it and would argue the toss and would eventually win.

So anyway going back to my pregnancy, very early on I realised to my horror that Trevor was a womaniser. There had been comments from him every now and then but I did not take any notice. He could not keep his eyes off women anywhere and everywhere and it was not just glances. He would often say that he always wanted to have children but still be a bachelor.

I thought I was loved for me and for me there would be nobody else. You are supposed to marry for life no matter what, till death do you part or so I believed. To make matters worse Jean his mum would always refer to Trevor's last girlfriend. At any opportunity, and she was mentioned time and time again.

Trevor was not good with responsibility, he was not really interested in the pregnancy and at times I felt shunned. His work was more important. On many occasions he made me feel that married life was not what he wanted. The baby coming into our lives was something to prove to him that he could father a child nothing else.

I would often ask myself why had he chosen for us to get married if this wasn't what he wanted. There was a bit of resentment when I would talk about the baby by name. I knew it would be a boy, and we had even named him, Steven.

Three weeks before the due date I started having contractions, my father-in-law drove me and Trevor to the hospital. They waited outside as I was being made ready to give birth as for some reason this was it, I was going to have our baby. I was happy, nervous and excited and so wished that my mum could have been with me. It took well over thirty-six hours and by this time Trevor thought it would still be ages so he and Terry went outside for a smoke, and at 11:00 pm, I gave birth to Steven he weighed 5lb 9oz.

The only person with me was the nurse who coached me through the pregnancy and gave me gas and air. The staff found Trevor and told him about his son. Being so late at night I could not talk to him properly, but he promised me he would ring my mum and dad and give them the news. Due to Steven coming into our world very early he was rushed by the staff and put into an incubator. I never got the chance to hold him.

It was such a lonely time, I will never forget it. Steven was seventeen days early and was in the incubator. It would be a few days before I could hold him and feed him myself. Being premature he was jaundiced, and at the time, babies could not go home until jaundice had subsided. I was in hospital for ten days, and at that time, my parents came down to visit and my two uncles came too.

As Trevor did not drive his dad would bring him or his brother Luke did once too. There was nothing to stop Trevor from getting a bus like I had done for the past nine months for my check-ups. I soon realised that Trevor was reluctant to use buses end of the story.

My uncle Victor was so gentle, kind and extremely patient. He would have made a wonderful Dad, and on many occasions, I would say to God, "Why couldn't he have been my dad?" Anyway, Uncle Victor was a gentle giant he was over six feet tall and weighed about twenty-four stone. He was so delighted and happy at seeing Steven I just could not believe his joy and how enamoured he was at Steven being so tiny. Good job too otherwise I would have had trouble. He and Uncle Charles came to visit me in the hospital twice.

I remember just after we got married Uncle Victor and Charles had come down to visit us in our new home, but really it was to take us to a department store in Maidstone to buy us some furniture. We ended up having a lovely sideboard with a dining table and chairs. Uncle Charles was not too happy at the expenditure, but I could see that Uncle Victor loved every minute of being able to buy us something lasting.

Anyway, I eventually went home to start my new life with our baby Son. I sat in the bedroom after bottle-feeding Steven and recollected that just a year before having him, I had changed my life through being married, moving home and having a new job along with the responsibilities of married life. The only thing I had ever been responsible for was my savings in the post office. Wow, so much in one go, it felt as though I had not had time to breathe, and I was being bounced from situation to situation.

Within a day of my being home with Steven, Trevor complained of not being well and went to bed, so I was up and down the stairs to him as well as Steven, he was well enough though for my mum and dad's visit a few days later, acting as though I was overreacting when telling them he had not been well.

Not even two months after Steven's birth I was making my usual weekly phone call to Mum and Dad, but this time 'hoorah' I was using the phone from our home in the luxury of our front room. To me, this was real luxury especially not having to stand in a smelly and cold phone box. Anyway, I was talking to my dad as per usual, and I asked about my mum, and then my uncles and dad was a bit funny. I thought Dad has had a row with them again.

Dad asked to speak to Trevor for a moment and told him that my uncle Victor had passed away about two weeks previous but that they did not want the shock to make me ill and asked if Trevor could tell me. Then Trevor put the phone down and told me.

OH MY GOD, I went ballistic. How could they do that to me? They had no conceivable idea how much Uncle Victor really meant to me. I was sobbing and crying so much I even scared Trevor.

Apparently, Uncle Victor had been admitted to hospital and developed pneumonia soon after and passed away, it was very quick. His funeral had already taken place, and I never got the chance to say goodbye. I could never forgive my parents for that.

We later found out Uncle Victor knew he was dying a year before he passed but chose not to tell us for fear of spoiling my wedding and then of course my pregnancy. That's why Uncle Victor was delighted at being able to see Steven. He must have hung on desperately so that he could see Steven. It now made sense to me, as when I would feed Steven at night, instead of drinking his milk he would look up in the space beside me and smile or giggle, and I would have to coax him to drink. I knew then it was Uncle Victor watching over him.

Uncle Victor was my haven when I needed help with my homework, he would sit with me for hours explaining everything in detail and making sure I was happy before going back up home. He would make me laugh with his jokes.

Although he did not play any musical instrument he would pick up the spoons and do the percussion bit whilst

Uncle Charles played the violin, and Dad played the accordion. They are the few happy times I remember when Nan and Uncles would come up for Easter or Christmas and music was played. Having said that it also meant that my mum bless her heart was working till late at night preparing the meals and confectionery for those delicious mealtimes.

I was never allowed to help only with dishing up and clearing away. I can understand her reasoning now because the kitchen was only twelve feet by ten feet. At those few gatherings, Dad would behave and act normal.

Uncle Victor was the one that calmed my dad down when Dad would go over the top with his temper. Uncle Victor would hear Dad ranting and shouting and fearing that he would hurt one of us he would quietly come up the stairs and in his quiet voice would call to my dad. Most times Dad would apologise to him for getting him concerned and that everything was alright, but on odd occasions, he would tell Uncle Victor to mind his own business and leave him alone.

The very sad thing about Uncle Victor was that as a young man he would be attracted to girls and tried to date them, but as soon as my Nan found out, she would make sure the girls were put off. One time, he got really serious about a young woman, and I think Mum said they even got engaged, but my Nan spoilt it all for them and the woman turned Uncle Victor down.

My Nan did not like women and was not happy when my dad married my mum. One day when I was a teenager, I had just finished helping Nan make the beds she turned to me and said, "Do you know you are a punishment from God?" I was shocked and could not answer, it was not until many years later that I found out I had been born out of wedlock plus I was a girl and that's what she had meant.

I would help my Nan with the beds, ironing, anything that she was struggling with. She, in turn, would offer me money which I would refuse, but at times, she did win, and I would buy saving stamps to stick in my Post Office savings book. I would then use this money to buy presents at Christmas.

There was a next-door neighbour at Mum and Dad's who was on her own and over the years had the odd conversation with Uncle Victor. When my Nan died the neighbour would invite Uncle Victor round for a coffee. It made me so happy, knowing that he was finally having female company. When he had passed away, Mum said a few weeks after the funeral on one of their visits to the cemetery they had found a bunch of flowers on the grave and presumed they were from the neighbour.

The extra sadness was that my parents never spoke to her about her friendship with Uncle Victor, as though their friendship had been a terrible thing. I would have been very happy to talk to her, but I would have suffered the wrath of my dad.

I have no doubt many of you will remember the early 70s when interest rates shot through the roof and many people lost their homes. For us, the interest rise happened six months after Steven was born. We were just about managing on one wage and Trevor was going up to London by car with his brother who had recently secured a job with a big computer firm in the centre of London.

With Trevor deciding to travel up to London with his brother Luke, Trevor was away from home for long hours. It was saving us money in train fares his brother Luke was not complaining because we paid for a tank of petrol once a week.

I would get up at 5:00 to make Trevor's sandwiches for work and get him a cup of tea before he went. He would be gone by 5:30 just in time for me to get Steven's feed ready for 6:00. Steven was always crying. He did not sleep long at nights any housework was done mostly with one hand as most of the time I carried him with the other arm.

I would try and take him out in the pram, and he still cried. He had colic a lot of the time, but he just cried most of the time. I would walk around for hours at night rocking him to sleep in my arms and as soon as I would put him down he would start again. In the end, he would start crying again, and I would cry too at not knowing why he was like it.

I had no help from Trevor only at weekends, as long as he wasn't working or going to play golf with his dad. I would ask the health visitor what could I do to help Steven, and she had run out of ideas. I would periodically get Steven checked over by the GP just in case he had missed something.

Teething just made him worse, and basically, Steven cried all the way through his first year and did not sleep through the night until he was nearly two years old.

One day, I was so desperate for some help, a break, anything. Steven had been crying all day, and I decided to put him in the pram and just walk the streets until I knew Trevor would be home. With Steven in the pram crying, and he just would not stop and all of a sudden for a split second I could have just walked out in front of the traffic and got us both killed just for some peace. I stopped in my tracks and it was like somebody tapping me on the shoulder, and I just cried with shame and horror.

It scared me so much that I ran home pushing the pram with Steven still crying. I cried my heart out when I got in, I was sobbing and for some reason that had stopped Steven from crying. For ages, after that, I would walk on the estate roads and never go near the main road for a long time.

I never admitted to anyone how evil I had been. Afterwards, for a very long time, I would do my shopping at the parade near home.

There was no solution to my anguish and desperation to make things better for Steven, but as long as he was in my arms, he was quiet until night-time.

With a mortgage and an endowment to boot, we were really in strife, and I decided that I should try and get a temping job in London near my parents in South London. This meant I would have to get up at 4:30 am run around getting feeds, sandwiches and everyone clothed for the 5:30 am pick up in the car. I was then dropped off at Sloan Square at around 7:30 am and then get a bus to Mum's drop Steven off and all his stuff and shoot off for another bus journey this time for half an hour to the temp job I had secured near Crystal Palace South London.

Sometimes, I was nearly late for the 9:00 start. I finished at 3:00 pm and the journeys would start all over again in reverse. Because we would arrive home after 7:00 pm I would feed Steven in the car on the way home and all I had to do when we got home was to wash him down and put him to bed. I would cook the meals at the weekend, and I would heat them every night for our evening meals.

I know that everyone, but the hardiest of you will agree that I could not do this for very long as something had to give. Yes, my health within six months I had to stop my efforts and put my health and our son first. Trevor did nothing to help as he felt he was working long hours and his job demanded more brain work.

Weekends, I spent catching up with everything whilst Trevor 'recharged his batteries'. Trevor had started as a clerk of works on building sites. Ever since we were married I would fetch and carry and do everything at home with very little input from Trevor. So I called time on my efforts of getting a job and stayed home and tried to recover and spend quality time with my son.

Not for long though, I 'encouraged' Trevor to look for work, which paid more. He was never good at pushing himself forward and by now my dad was on my back going on about how Trevor should fight to get a better-paid job and that with a family you don't leave it to the woman to help you in this matter. For once in my life, my dad said something nice in my favour.

Then Trevor's mum suggested I might like to go strawberry picking with some of her neighbours. I'll try anything I thought, so we got picked up in a van at 8:00 am and finished at 3:00 pm. I worked like the clappers with Steven in the buggy at the end of the row crying and not liking the experience at all. The girls were not happy because I worked too fast and made them look bad and with Steven crying all the time he made me stop more times than I wanted to, but I persevered.

By the time strawberry picking was finished, I looked like a brown berry, a very similar colour to when I first came to England. This time everyone was admiring my tan. Then came the hop training which made your hands all brown and took ages to come off, but Steven still cried most of the time and the girls were getting fed up with us, so I packed it in.

A few months on Trevor had got a better-paid job so we approached a mortgage company in order to change our present arrangement and get rid of the endowment that had been a condition for us to get our first mortgage. That endowment had been a real millstone around our necks.

Once everything was finalised life got somewhat a bit easier financially. I still wanted to contribute because Trevor never stopped making me feel that I was a lady of leisure and not doing my bit. I got myself eggs delivered at home from the local farm and using the pram chassis I would put the large box of eggs in it and go round the houses in the evenings selling them. At times, it would pour down with rain, and I'd only manage to sell a couple of dozen.

Trevor did not object because Steven would already be in bed by then. I did not make much money and Trevor was not always home early enough for me to do it. I also tried selling make-up door to door but that failed too. When you don't have the support behind you, it is very hard to succeed. Something I could never be accused of not giving Trevor.

Some of the neighbours in our road had babies too and there were three of us with very young children roughly the same age and sometimes I would get invited for a cup of tea. They were seasoned Mothers as they had older children and these were the last of their brood. I found it difficult to gel with them, I had not had friends before let alone been invited into their homes. I was on ceremony all the time and petrified that Steven would break or mess something up.

Chris the elder of the two mums was so blaze about everything. She reminded me of people who lived on farms and let their kids do what they want. She was always telling me to relax, lighten up, children have to learn.

I wasn't in and out of their houses like they were with each other, I had jobs to do indoors and the house had to be clean and dinner cooked for when Trevor got home. I was like my mum had been with us, and I cooked everything from scratch. I didn't want Trevor to think I was skiving all day. I had to justify all those hours on my own with Steven as Trevor had already accused me of on several occasions of being a woman of leisure. Flippin' 'eck, it felt just like when I was at home, and Dad would never believe anything I said.

One day I frequented another woman who lived further up the road, and she had a thirteen-year-old daughter who I was introduced to. Melisa was blond very pretty and slim and loved Steven. She volunteered to sit for us any time we wanted to go out. I nearly laughed in her face.

We had only gone out once in the two and a half years of being married and that was a year after Steven was born and Jean Trevor's mum had sat for us. We had only gone out for a meal just up the road.

Melisa started coming over at times just before Trevor was due home. She was not very tactful and stayed whilst I was trying to get Steven for bed and preparing our dinner. Trevor did not complain because he spent all his time coming home talking to Melisa and charming her something rotten. She lapped up all the attention and it made me sick to watch.

After a few months, I could not stand it anymore. I told Melisa that she should come over for visits straight from school as her visits at teatime meant that I did not get any help from Trevor. She wasn't happy but agreed.

Just over two years after Steven was born I was pregnant again, but this time, the pregnancy was totally different as I was feeling unwell. I knew what it was, after Steven was born Trevor had bullied me into going on the pill this was very much against my feelings, and at the time, I was really nervous.

The pill made me lose a lot of weight and when we thought the time was right I'd stopped taking it. I was soon pregnant and feeling ill, lethargic and crying a lot. I felt as though everything inside me was wrong.

I had gone to the GP at the beginning of my pregnancy with troubles and losing blood, he turned to me and said, "You must prepare yourself that your baby will not be normal and it will have problems." I was so upset and felt it was my entire fault because I had relented and gone on the pill. The GP had said that it was probably the pill still in my system, and we had not waited long enough after stopping the pill and trying to get pregnant.

The pregnancy with my lovely daughter Alice was so fraught with visits by ambulance to the hospital. My body was rejecting her, and on one occasion, I nearly lost her. Complete rest said the Doctor, I nearly laughed in his face. I was getting no help from Trevor's family, my parents were too far away, and Trevor was making sure he worked all the hours he could manage.

I must remind you at this point before you say to yourself well he was bringing in extra money, NO Trevor never got overtime, whether he worked seven hours a day or eighty hours a week. As I have told you already, Trevor was not good with responsibility unless it was work. Gradually, as time went on, I was responsible for more, and more things until before our seventh anniversary, I was managing everything at home.

I lost count of how many times I was admitted to the hospital where my body was threatening to miscarry our baby Alice. I knew she was going to be a girl, and we named her too before she was born.

I would be admitted and put on a drip and given chemicals to stop the contractions. Then after a day or so I would be allowed home. All the time, I was worried if Steven was being looked after properly.

Steven was left with either a neighbour or depending on the time of day I was admitted he would be with my in-laws until Trevor got home. Everyone around me was getting fed up with this pregnancy (what about me I thought). Steven was a treasure and such a helpful child like no other.

Eventually, the due date was a week away and at my last hospital check-up, it was discovered that my baby was quite large, and I may have trouble giving birth. Oh great, I thought it wasn't enough that I had gone through the whole of the pregnancy thinking that my baby would not be normal in some way, now I was being told of more problems and that I may have to be induced.

I thought no way Jose, and in that last week, I worked like a Trojan, ate hot foods, anything to make me have my baby naturally and no more chemicals. My Alice was due on the same due date Steven had been due, but he was born seventeen days early and Alice came three days before her due date. What a relief, and she came really quickly five hours, and she was with us. Yes, I say with us as it was a Saturday and Trevor was home.

He had decided that he would be at the birth and this filled me with trepidation as I did not think he would be able to cope. He had been hyped up by his sister's husband telling him that a lot of fathers were at their baby's births. I was so relieved that all had gone well and Alice was a perfect baby. She was not that big and weighed just one pound more than Steven.

I thanked God, the universe, my Guardian Angel and my ancestors that day so many times. If I had listened to the GP and his prediction about Alice, we could have decided to abort a healthy baby.

After two days, I was home, and this time, I knew what I had to do and Steven was a treasure. He would watch over his little sister, alerting me when she stirred, helping with the feeds and nappy changing. By now from different conversations I'd had with Mum on our previous visits Mum realised that when Alice was born I would need help. Dad agreed to let Mum come and stay with us for a few days and help me with the children.

Good job too as Trevor was back at work the day after I got home. My mum was in her element as she was free of Dad and his domineering. This was the first time in my life (twenty-three years) that I was able to have face to face conversations with Mum and Dad was not there to interrupt or put his 'two penneth in'.

Within a few days, Dad came to collect Mum for their journey back to London by coach, I was so sad to see her go, her piece of freedom had gone. For the first time, I was starting to bond with my mum and it felt so nice. Both of us welling up and each knowing what the other was feeling. Alice had been a good baby from day one, and I was so pleased that Mum was there to calm my fears as Alice had been the complete opposite to Steven.

Steven had cried all the time for the first two years, but Alice was content, she would have her feeds and would sleep. As time went on she would sleep for longer, and within a couple of weeks, she was sleeping right through the night. On the first night it happened, I woke up looking at the clock and nudged her thinking she may be ill. She was fine and soon ready for her feed. I wanted to be reassured so I went to see the GP, and when I asked him to check Alice over and told him why, he laughed and said I had got a contented baby and that she was fine.

I went home as happy as Larry because I could now think of moving Alice in with Steven as she would not be interrupting his sleep at night.

Trevor's parents were getting fed up living up the road from us and decided to move three miles down the road in an old three-bed semi, Luke his brother was still living at home and helped out with the purchase and the mortgage of the property.

Steven by now was clean and able to attend nursery school and loved it. This would give me some time with Alice and make a fuss of her. After a while, Steven would pick up the usual childhood illnesses, and on several occasions, Alice would be affected too. I remember one time Steven caught chickenpox and Alice too.

Confinement for this childhood illness was that you had to stay home until the last scab fell off. As I was home coping with the children on my own as nobody would come near you in those days for fear of their own children catching chickenpox. One day I had run out of most items of food at home and there wasn't enough to make a meal.

Trevor would be home late after the shops had shut so I waited until it was dark about five, clothed the children really warm and snug and with Steven sitting on top of the pram away from Alice's feet I quickly ran to the shops in the village where nobody knew me and therefore would not come close to see the children. I left Alice and Steven outside and ran around like Anika Rice grabbing items for our meal and within minutes I was back with the children and rushing home again. Steven loved the pram ride there and back and would ask me to go faster.

Weekends were never very special because Trevor wanted to stay home and relax, and I did the housework seven days a week and the gardening. At times, Trevor's dad would invite him to play a round of golf and not having been associated with golfing I thought they would be back within two to three hours. They would go early morning and not come back until the middle or late afternoon.

When Steven and Alice were quite young I would read constantly to them and it was partly my excuse to learn the stories English children had learnt from childhood and to do something with them that I had missed out on too. I had missed out on all of that normal English growing up because having been born abroad and my parents never read to me anyway. I was desperate to give my two children the same start in life other children were experiencing with their English parents.

As Alice got older before she had started nursery, she would sit with me and would read to me one of her ladybird books. She had remembered the story from the pictures and used them as prompts and remembered some of the words in the storyline—and would read me the story. It was lovely to hear her. At times I would catch her sitting on the floor with her dolls around her and reading her ladybird books to them.

(Whilst I was in the process of writing this book it was my birthday and Steven said he would visit me with some lunch—Chinese as I love it. Melisa my twenty-one-year-old granddaughter came with him. I was also given a bunch of flowers and a small buttercream cake. We ate our meal whilst chatting and trying to catch up, and I kept looking at Melisa thinking my how she has grown up and Steven suddenly jumped up and said, "Oh Mum, I've left your card in the car." When I opened the card, I started to cry. The card was a cover from a Ladybird book titled, *The World's Best Mum*, the title really got me so emotional because you will find out later why.

I thanked him so much, but I could not hug him due to the COVID-19 virus. My Angels had sent me their message 'the card' telling me that I was doing the right thing by writing the book. I also explained to Steven and Melisa why I had got so emotional).

Having had two younger brothers made it difficult for me to have conversations about dolls and storybooks. I do have a photo that tells me I would have looked at books with my brother Albert as he was five years younger than me, but I don't recollect it. My childhood was so filled with fear and anxiety that I remember most of the bad things and only some good bits, isn't that an awful thing to say? I was under pressure all the time trying to do the right thing and not make my dad or mum angry.

It was so rewarding to see Steven and Alice do more things as they were growing up and their little characters were forming. If I remember correctly the first words for both of them were Dad.

A couple of years on and Trevor was approached by a building company for him to join them. The money was better, and they offered a company car too. At the time, Trevor did not drive but had driven off-road in his dad's car on several occasions before we got married.

Trevor signed up with a local driving school and within weeks had passed his test and had his licence. He approached his boss and told him that he now had a driving licence, and he got his first company car.

When we were still living in our first home, Trevor would walk around the site in Wapping East London doing his inspection and making sure the work was going to schedule as the Clerk of Works. He would always find nails, screws, hooks that had been discarded by the workforce, and he would pick some up and bring them home. This got to be a habit and when he got home before taking his jacket off he would empty the pocket on the table (Like a child coming home from school and picking up something in the street).

On one very large site that he was the clerk of works, Trevor had brought home two items. Apparently, many years before the war, there had been a fairground on the site. On this particular day, as Trevor emptied his pockets he said, "Look what I found, the digger brought some stuff up today," and as he handed it to me thinking it was a special nail or a clay pipe or something, it was a little lead soldier, the paint on it hardly recognisable and it was missing a leg. As the soldier touched my hand I took my hand away and it fell to the floor.

I felt such deep sadness, and I cried for quite a while. Trevor stood looking at me bewildered and then proceeded to show me a dinner fork. "NO, no, no, no, you can't bring these things home. People have died that had these things you must promise me to put them back where you found them and let them be buried where they lay, please I beg you." After that episode, Trevor was very reluctant to bring anything home.

I really cannot remember how long it was from that horrible experience that I could feel a presence in the bedrooms upstairs. I was sure that it was not there to hurt us, but I'd felt very uncomfortable knowing there was an energy in the bedrooms. I mentioned it to Trevor, and he could feel nothing. The children were fine and slept well at night.

All I could tell was that it was an old man with very similar features to my dad's dad who I had never known only from pictures; because I felt uncomfortable I did not think it was family. This feeling went on for a few days and going up the stairs during the day when the children were at school and playgroup I would find it difficult to climb the stairs to tidy up. Visits to the bathroom were easier as the stairs were in a straight line to the door and the presence was only in the two bedrooms, but I would always hurry back down the stairs.

Then one evening, Trevor and I were watching television, and I felt really scared and threatened as though I was going to die, a fear I had never experienced (Our backs were on the wall of the staircase and the lounge door was at right angles to the front door). I literally felt the energy come down the stairs and out the door. As it went, I felt drained and relieved, and I was able to go up to the children after that with no problem. One thing that I had done that day was to talk to the spirit/soul with my mind and say that I was not able to help him, and I was very sad and could he please find someone who could.

The very few holidays we did have were always marred by Trevor admiring and ogling the 'scenery' and I don't mean the sea or countryside. I felt so lonely and neglected and that I was just a commodity, something he could have as and when he felt like it. Never any compliments or even noticing what I was wearing.

At one point he even told me that wearing makeup did not suit me and to please him hoping he would show some love I stopped wearing it. My parents would make comments about this, but I never said why.

There was very little love between us, and I would write Trevor notes and put them in his lunch box. I would tell him how unhappy and unloved I felt and that it would be nice to get a bit of attention. When I would ask if he had found my note his replies would be, silence or ignoring me completely or saying that he was really busy and did not realise that was how I felt.

Hence, nothing ever changed, so knowing that this was my lot seven years into my marriage I just had to get on with it for the sake of my children. It may seem cruel, but the children were more mine than 'ours' because it never interested him to get involved in their upbringing, only if he felt like it.

If I wanted to go grocery shopping and needed to leave the children with him he would bring up excuses and in the end I'd got so fed up with his excuses I would get everything ready should he need nappies etc. and go, he couldn't have it all his way. It would have been no good asking Trevor to go shopping instead as he had never done any.

His mum once told me that she had sent Trevor to the butcher for some stewing steak and when asked by the butcher what he would like Trevor's reply was, "I'll have a pound of English." They all had a good laugh at the time.

All our troubles started really after Steven was born and no matter what I did to try and encourage Trevor to be more loving or attentive towards me it did not work. He was jealous of the attention I was giving Steven. I would always have to put on an act so that the children did not notice how unhappy I was. Sometimes I could not hide the hurtful way I was treated. There were no loving touchy feeling moments, it all came from me.

I would even have to ask for a hug or cuddle or even a kiss. Very quickly even before Alice was born we were just like housemates and not much else. Well, housemates with a perk for him. I felt at times that my father-in-law knew what was in store for me with Trevor, only I never got paid for my services.

The few holidays we did have I did for the children. History was repeating itself once again, just like when my family had our holidays. This time though there was no shouting just the silence and ignoring which was just as bad. We always did what he suggested and it made life a lot easier. My two lovely children were going to have a family life without the hassles that I'd had with my dad no matter what sacrifices I had to make.

Alice was by now at playgroup and Steven was now at junior school, but we were having problems with Steven's class teacher and because the situation could not be resolved, we decided to change his school to one just around the corner.

Ashford Kent

Steven was just settling into his new school when we decided to move to a bigger house on a new housing estate further along the coast near Ashford Kent. This meant that both of the children would be going to the local village school two miles away in Great Chart. They each had their own bedrooms and my parents and Trevor's parents could come to stay for the weekend.

Steven thrived, and later Alice entered the infants. The walk from our newly built four-bedroom home was a long walk across fields, down the country lane to the main road and the long walk leading up the steep hill to the village school. On Alice's first day at school, I was walking home crying. I was so nervous for her and worried she might not like her school dinners, also it was another big change for me again.

In the four years, we lived in our new home I can count on one hand how many times Trevor went to school. If I had the misfortune to invite one of the teachers Trevor would be charming them or chatting them up to the point that they would make an early exit. I had joined the PTA and was a Teacher's Helper. I then volunteered as a kitchen/lunchtime assistant.

I was with the children a lot and it stopped me from getting bored and lonely at home. The one thing that really hurt—many years on and I don't know why she had to tell me—Alice and I were having a conversation about her first days at school, and I explained how sad I'd felt at leaving her crying and even sobbing and her not wanting to be left. She turned to me and said that she had done that to make me feel bad, but as soon as my back was turned, she was as right as rain. I was stunned and shocked and only she knew why she'd had to be like that.

We had chosen a four-bedroom property newly built on a new housing estate outside the main town so that when my parents came to visit they could stay for a day or two, and my mum and I could have a good chat. Mum loved it, but Dad was not happy not knowing whether Trevor's dad would suddenly turn up out of the blue.

Dad liked his routine and was not prepared to give it up for anyone. In the four years we lived there Mum and Dad only ever managed one overnight visit.

As Trevor now had a company car I would choose to go up to Mum and Dad's in London whenever the children had a break at school. Trevor would take us in the car as far as South London and by bus for the rest of the journey. It made it a very long day for the children and me, but Trevor was used to it. Trevor would meet us at Mum and Dads' when he finished work.

After we'd all had dinner, we would make our way home. The children were always spoilt by Mum we always brought home so much, food, toys and more.

Having the bigger house gave me the opportunity to have students in the spare room, and we put bunk beds in and would have up to four students at a time. It was funny when we had French students because I would not divulge my being fluent in French, I would listen to them on their first day to see what they thought of us. It was quite funny to see their faces when afterwards they heard me talk in French.

I made sure that we spoke English the best part of the time as they were here after all to learn English. It would be good also for Steven and Alice to meet children from other nations.

In the time that I was registered to have students we had, one seventeen-year-old German boy—three Italian girls— four French boys and a partridge in a pear tree (no sorry I couldn't resist, for a while it sounded like I was reciting the twelve days of Christmas).

As I said we were in the house for four years, and we had health problems. Alice was very sick one day, and we weren't sure if she'd had mild symptoms of meningitis. Steven did not seem to be affected, I had flu-like symptoms a lot of the time and lost quite a lot of weight and had a nervous breakdown.

Trevor caught meningitis, the one that you cannot be given drugs for and was rushed to the William Harvey hospital five miles away and was put in isolation for about a week and given a lumbar puncture. It took him months to get back to reasonable health and to start a full day's work again.

Whilst we were there we also managed to build a huge patio area at the back with three feet high raised borders, a rockery and a stone wall all around the front garden finished off with wrought iron front and side gate. I did a lot of the brickwork for the raised border of the large patio, and I was spotted doing this by two bricklayers in the next garden. They shouted over to see if I wanted a job as they were impressed with my work.

By the second year, we were on the new estate more families had moved in and more children were going to the village school in Great Chart. Very quickly in the mornings, there would be five of us mums with all our children walking through the fields and up to the school. Sometimes we would all have tea or coffee in one of our houses and then go home to our housework. I was the only one without a car so on wet days Steven and Alice would travel to school in one of the Mums' cars.

With more women around Trevor was so attentive to them if they happen to come over for a chat. He was really keen on a new Mum who had moved in, and I could feel the energy from him to her and likewise. It hurt so much. Standing near them watching them chat each other up.

Trevor was encouraged by the local conservative officer to stand for the local council for the new estate where hundreds of new homes were being built. I supported him 100% and canvassed with leaflets for the weeks leading up to the election. It was something Trevor really wanted, and I gave all my support. I was by now well known in the village as one of the PTA members, and I would help at any village event.

At the same time, as Trevor was standing for the elections, the Parish council in the village were looking for someone to fill a vacancy on their council, someone who would represent the new residents on the estate. I was approached but declined and explained why. It was pointed out to me that it would only mean one meeting a month. So I said I would help them out but did not know what was really involved, besides which I did not know that many people.

The elections came and Trevor had gone with his colleague from the party to the Polling station and later on to wait for the results. Trevor came home so upset, he'd lost by seven votes and unbeknown to me until the following day when I got the phone call, I got in with a majority of seven votes. I was distraught, I had not wanted the job, I knew that I would not get any support from home and it would mean extra work.

Trevor pretended to be happy, but I could see that he was annoyed at me getting through and not canvassing and here he was having worked so hard with the canvassing, and he had lost out (I think Trevor was having a selective memory moment, but I'd worked my socks off too even when he was at work I had been canvassing for him).

Trevor gave me a hard time whenever I mentioned that I had the Parish meeting and would either be home late which made me late going or he had work to do and would not look after the children properly. My only way of getting there because he would not drive me was by my using Steven's bicycle, he was by now ten and nearly as tall as me (five feet). It was ok going but cycling through the fields at night was no joke and a bit scary. In the end, after a year of struggling to meet my pledge, I had to surrender my position, delighting Trevor no end.

Throughout his career Trevor moved from one company to another each one approaching him for his expertise of the construction industry, then once the contract was finished another job came up. As he got older and more knowledgeable he was moving up the ladder and at times worked for the client or the contractor in top management.

Steven was looking forward to going to secondary school and the options we had in our area were not good. It was for this reason and the fact that Trevor had secured another good job in London that we reluctantly chose to move so that Trevor could have a more direct route to London as we could not guarantee his having a car with every company he worked for.

Crawley West Sussex

So in 1984, we found a three-bed semi in Crawley West Sussex which gave us access to the London to Brighton Railway Service. This also made it easier for Mum and Dad to visit as they were used to travelling to Brighton by train for days out. The schools had a lot more to offer the children and Trevor had easy access to the M23 and M25. Me? I just fitted in with all the changes no problem!

After a while, I got quite friendly with all the elderly neighbours who had grandchildren Steven and Alice's age. As Steven and Alice were very polite and well behaved, they were a great hit with all the neighbours. We lived in that house for twenty years.

When we moved to our Crawley house, Steven started his last year at junior school and Alice was in infants. I would have to walk past Alice's school grounds to get to the small shopping parade that was opposite Steven's school.

The children were very happy and eased themselves into schoolwork quite well. Steven's progress was good and the secondary school he would be going to with most of his classmates was just at the back of our house. The main road at the back of the house provided good access to Gatwick and further on.

With Trevor having good access to the M23 and M25, he was home at times so early that it seemed strange for all of us to have our evening meal together. Finally, we were settling down to contented family life after eleven years of being watched and criticised by Trevor's family.

After a couple of years at our new home, Alice was by now at junior school and Steven at Secondary school. They were both coming home on their own and it gave me time to indulge in driving lessons.

Trevor was always moaning or giving me the excuse that he was tired when I would ask to visit my parents which was a sixty-mile round trip about an hour to hour and a half away. I wanted my parents and the children to have the chance of enjoying each other's company before Steven and Alice got too independent and stopped wanting to visit Mum and Dad regularly.

On many occasions, I would have dreams that I was driving along a road and it seemed so natural. I started learning to drive, and I just could not fathom out why it all had to be so complicated with gear shifts etc. I eventually took my test and failed. I then decided to learn in an automatic and bingo I passed.

Trevor pointed out to me that I would be restricted to driving just automatics and I'd shrugged my shoulders saying "who cares?" I had not told him, but I wanted to drive so that in the future I would buy a second-hand car and be able to visit my parents without having to beg or make deals with him.

Our next-door neighbours (not the semi to ours) were a young family with young children, but unbeknown to any of us, they were from a large family who were constantly in trouble with the law.

One night I woke up with the sound of crackling and the flickering of what looked like a big bonfire. I got up quickly fearing the large tree outside the house had somehow caught light I opened the curtain to find Trevor's company car alight and within seconds the fuel tank blew. We called the fire brigade and police. I am sorry, but I shall cut this long story short. After looking through the debris, the police said that the fire had been started deliberately.

A few months later, Trevor's other company car was broken into and all his work papers stolen, together with the radio his parking money from the dashboard, they had managed to get in via the passenger rear window. This time the culprits were caught and the Police found that a visitor living with those same neighbours next door was responsible for the break-in, and they found all the car contents in the bedroom cupboard. I was so upset.

It was Alice's last day at junior school and secondary school was beckoning. I decided to give her and her school friends a barbeque party in the back garden. Not wishing to upset our elderly residents in the street I wrote to six three either side of us and explained what we were planning and hoped that there would not be too much noise and it would all be finished by 9:00 pm.

All of Alice's school friends came round and the party was a great hit especially when I played their favourite music. Alice had come home that day with her school blouse autographed by her school friends and teachers and was beaming. She too had constantly been bullied at school but on this day she was a hit with everyone including the neighbours, as nobody complained and the next-door neighbour was at her top floor window for a lot of the time enjoying the music and listening to their chatter.

As Alice and Steven were growing up, I wanted to try and get them used to different Nations' meals. So from time to time, I would have a week where I would cook a different meal from a different country.

Pizza, Pasta al Forno, Turkey Curry, Roast Beef, Chicken Kiev, Chicken Stir Fry, Tuna Rice Salad (my mum would make that for us when we were young). They enjoyed all the meals, but Trevor needed more convincing and persuading so he would have English food. Both Alice and Steven have grown up being more adventurous with their meals and are both now very good cooks at home.

I was home a lot of the time and nearly always home by the time Steven and Alice got home from school. I started suffering from severe headaches and feeling sick and it would not go away. On days that I was home most especially in the winter, I was even more unwell. For some reason, one of the neighbours mentioned they were getting their boiler serviced by a very reliable chap and it suddenly dawned on me that having been in the property for nearly five years we had not had our boiler serviced.

At the time, I thought Trevor should have thought about this. I got the chap to come round and service the boiler that sat in a corner of the kitchen. He took one look and asked me if I had been feeling ill at all, and I replied 'yes'. He proceeded to tell me that I was being poisoned with carbon monoxide gasses from the boiler and that I could have died.

One day when Steven and Alice were young teenagers and still relatively happy to go out with us we decided to go to Bognor Regis. Trevor had got a Cavalier company car, and we were off. We walked around the town and as we passed a Morrisons supermarket in the precinct so we did some shopping and then came home.

A while after getting home I got the big map out and searched for the place where the Morrisons supermarket was in relation to the rest of the town. I was looking and tracing with my finger the route we had taken and found the 'M' I had been looking for and then suddenly I found another and another, and with joy, I shouted out, "Great, there are loads of Morrisons dotted all around this area."

We will be able to shop in one again. Steven came over and looked and burst out laughing so loudly that it brought Trevor and Alice in to see what was so funny. I was hurt and bemused, Steven told them that I had found numerous Morrisons on the map, but they were really 'Museums', doh! Steven hugged me and said, "I do love you, Mum." I felt so bloody stupid.

Over the years occasionally I had kept my hand in typing for agencies on a part-time basis. Also for a number of years Trevor would come home late from a meeting and had notes or minutes to type up for the following day, so whilst he was having his evening meal that would sometimes be around 10:00 pm, I would be typing up his notes. He would read through them, and we would make corrections, and we could finally go to bed on many instances around 1:00 am.

When the word processors came out I was really keen to use them so that I would be able to get a part-time job and also be quicker at typing up Trevor's site notes. We bought one, and I asked Trevor to help me learn how to use it, but he would leave out some of the instruction or things to watch for he would blind me with science, and I struggled like mad to learn the process and I'd got so furious with myself for being so inept and stupid. Due to my tenacity, I had finally mastered it and realised what Trevor had done, and I was so annoyed with him. It had been his way of stopping me from getting more efficient.

The word processor was a boon because it helped me type things faster, and I could keep copies and there was no longer carbon paper to contend with. As Trevor's jobs got more demanding and involved this 'night-time' typing was becoming a regular occurrence, but Trevor never realised that had it not been for me giving him all that support and saving him hours of two-finger typing he would not have managed.

The offices had typists, but Trevor refused to improve his handwriting 'which literally looked like the muddy trail of a small spider', so he was asked to type up the notes himself and you can bet your bottom dollar that nobody knew it was me doing all the typing. Trevor was always too ready to take the credit.

Trevor's company car was always a manual, not that it had to be, but it gave him the chance to show that I still had to rely on him for visits to my parents and that having an automatic licence was still a hindrance rather than an advantage. He reminded me so much of my dad and the way Dad was with my mum wanting to be in control all the time.

I wouldn't mind it, but Trevor was not expected to do anything when we got there and my parents treated him like a lord. Mum would cook his favourite meals. Most time he would greet them have a bit of a chat with Dad and then he would get Dad's paper and be lost in that for a while.

Nothing was freely given by Trevor I always felt that I had to make it up to him. When we returned home that would be his job done. He would do nothing for the rest of the weekend and enjoy his leisure time.

On one occasion we were driving along Streatham High Street, and we got to a zebra crossing and Trevor stopped and the car behind smacked into the back of us. I jumped out of my seat and went to confront the driver, I told her my children were in the back, and she should remember to keep her distance. "Do you hear me?" I shouted at her. I have never been a violent person or wanted to hurt anybody but where my children were concerned that was different.

Another year or so went by and Trevor's dad had a major heart attack, and we went down to see them in Kent. It took Terry some time to recover and because their house was on a steep hill and the gardens were in steep stages at the back they decided to move. I could have bet my life on it that they would move closer to Trevor's sister further up the Kent coast. Instead, they moved about seven miles from us on the route to Brighton where Jean Trevor's mum had one of her Sisters living with her husband a retired salesman.

Before they had moved down, Luke had got himself a German Shepherd bitch and as the children were still quite young, I would worry at her reaction to them. I was told that German Shepherds were one-person dogs and very protective. I am glad to say we never had any problems.

Jean had wanted to be near her sister and her darling son, Trevor. Their new house was just around the corner from Jean's sister but was a steep hill walk to the shops in the village.

For most of my married life, I was teased and belittled by Trevor's sister about my London accent and how common I sounded. Trevor's family thought they were above everybody else. Jean's sister was the worse and when Jean and Terry and Luke moved near her, they ended up being treated as a poor relation and Jean as being common (What's the saying—what goes around comes around).

One time that Trevor was driving us to my parents I had been feeling uneasy about the journey and did not know why then I'd asked Trevor what route he would be taking as sometimes we would travel near Redhill Airport. On this particular trip, I persuaded him not to take the Redhill route, and to my amazement, my instincts were right as a plane had crashed on landing.

For a number of years the children had been on at us about getting a dog, and I refused because I knew that it would fall on me to do all the hard work. As the children were now in their teens I felt it was time they could take responsibility in looking after a dog or a cat and would take it in turns to walk them (the dogs not the cat). I had contacted the RSPCA and said that we were looking for a puppy and not too large a breed.

A few weeks later, on 2 March 1990, after a successful home check, I was contacted by the home saying that they had got five puppies ready for adoption four dogs and one bitch all from one litter. They had been left in a cardboard box by the side of the motorway.

I had already told the children that the dogs would be brothers and their names were Max and Sam. My instincts had already prepared me for their arrival, and to me, it felt like bringing home more children. Everyone was overjoyed and so looking forward to bringing them home (Oh yes, they had to be two I could not bear to think of just bringing one home alone).

They were ten weeks old and had been given a clean bill of health. We were allowed into the pen and Steven picked up Max and Alice tried to pick Sam up but dropped him and then picked him up again.

Max looked like a scruffy haired little rat all skin and bones and appeared to be the runt of the litter as all the others looked like Sam who was typical Labrador and chunky. They travelled home really well no whimpering and no accidents on the children's laps either.

Thinking back to my 'dog experiences', when I was about ten years old my dad out of the blue brought home from work a sandy coloured ball of fluff who we called Sandy. A workmate had puppies at home he wanted to get rid of. He was such a bouncy happy chap and peed everywhere, the dog not the bloke. He'd dug up the garden leaving big holes everywhere, much to the delight of Louis and Albert as they would play in these pits with their diggers and trucks.

Within a few months, he was making friends with the neighbours by holding himself up on the six-foot fence and barking and wagging his tail. He seemed to like the neighbours more than us. Eventually, he was too much for Mum to cope with, and we offered him to the neighbours. They were overjoyed and very happy to have him.

As we'd had one dog there was no reason why Mum and Dad could not contemplate another but a much smaller one. Dad asked around at work and within the year we had a German Shepherd cross who was black with brown patches, we called him Prince. He was a lively little fella and always tugging at his lead and bouncing around but gorgeous with it.

One outing with Prince I remember quite vividly, the whole family and Prince had gone to the local park, and we had taken a picnic. My brothers and I were running around with Prince and making him chase us, the picnic was by then ready for us to eat. Laid out on a lovely table cloth was an array of food Mum had prepared and with the food was a bowl of shelled hard-boiled eggs.

Prince took one look at them and dived into the bowl sending a few up in the air whilst he started chomping at each egg in turn, as though thinking that if he had bitten a piece out of each they would be his to finish. We all laughed so much but stopped him from eating the rest in case they made him ill.

On another occasion, I was on my way to collect my youngest brother Albert from junior school, and we were about a third of the way there when suddenly Prince started acting very strange and growling then whimpering. Thrashing about and frothing at the mouth, I was so scared for Prince I was crying and eventually sobbing as I could not calm him down. I was so worried that I would be late collecting Albert and Mum did not know what was going on. One of the residents in the street heard the commotion and called the police and the next thing I know they arrive with protective gloves and a noose to take Prince off me.

The police took Prince to the nearest vet, and I was driven to Albert's school, and we were both driven home. My dad rang the vet that evening to find that Prince had been put to sleep because his condition was distemper, and he could not be saved. It broke my heart.

Max and Sam were crossed with Labrador, and they thought a large hound possibly Irish Wolf Hound, but the home thought they would only be smallish. On our visits to Trevor's parents, all three dogs would play quite well and no fuss.

In the late 80s to early 90s, I had managed to get temp jobs whilst the children were at school, and I would rush back before the children got home. I was getting really concerned at how Steven was having sneaky drinks with his mates.

I had told Trevor that we needed to introduce both Steven and Alice to alcohol at home with us, I didn't want them trying alcohol with friends and perhaps get themselves in trouble or very ill. Trevor had been collecting miniature drink bottles for years and the walls in the dining room were full of them housed on small wooden slatted display shelving.

One weekend we all sat down and opened the most common drinks, whisky, gin, vodka and so on. At the third drink we offered them, Alice decided that she'd had enough and was feeling sick. Steven was eager to try them but was not keen on any. His favourite drink was larger. We talked to both of them about the health dangers of drink and how it can ruin lives and not just their own.

Both of them were grateful for the experience and said they would go back to school and tell their friends and teachers that they had been plied with strong alcohol by their parents that weekend. You just can't win, can you?

The next company Trevor worked for he was offered a car and travel expenses all taxed of course, but firstly, it meant that as Trevor this time opted for an automatic I was insured to drive it and if he was away for a day or two I could use it. It was heaven as on occasions I was independent.

When Steven and Alice were still at school and the conservatory was finished and the flooring had been finished (we did it ourselves as we ran out of money) I took the children, and we drove to the nearest garden centre and bought a huge Christmas tree to go in the conservatory. It was a good job the car was a hatchback, I had to buy some string in the centre too as the tree went right from the dashboard and about two feet out the back.

Steven and Alice could not stop laughing and were excited at the prospect of decorating the tree and more importantly that it would fit, and hopefully, we would not have to cut the top. With the garden centre under three miles away, I made sure the journey was safe for all of us including the tree.

Well we never measured either the space it was going to occupy or the tree itself—we got home, and we had to cut twelve inches off the top. It was a very spindly piece at the top so it did not affect the glorious splendour of the tree. We've recollected that story time and time again with smiles on all our faces.

At that time also, Steven had passed his exams at school and Alice was doing well at secondary school. Most of us will remember the 80s for the crash of the building industry and Trevor was out of work on three separate occasions in that decade. At the end of the 80s, Steven had chosen to attend a university in Wales to take Geology. Financially it was the worse time for us, but we backed Steven all the way and managed to get a grant to help with the fees (From both sides of the family Steven was the first to attend University and it was a bit like watching the Waltons when John boy leaves home for University) but Steven had also started going out with a girl from the other side of Crawley, and she was at University in another part of Wales.

So Trevor decided to hire a minibus and take all their possessions and drive them over for the beginning of their next academic year. I could not go because there was not enough room for the boys to join us and the journey would be too long for them cramped in the minibus without a break.

About five years after Trevor's family moved near Brighton Terry's emphysema was getting worse, and he was forced to give up smoking and use an oxygen mask. Jean was not very good at nursing and it would get her down, so she would get collected by Lynda and taken to hers for a week away. Terry never complained but gradually got worse and in the end because of all her efforts nursing Terry it was affecting Jean's health Terry went into the local hospital for a rest bite and Jean went to stay with Lynda for another break.

I felt it was sad that he had been put in there as he hardly had any visitors. I had taken it upon myself to visit him, and he would constantly ask where was the rest of the family. I would make all types of excuses to him hoping he would believe me. The journey was not easy as I had to take a train from Three Bridges and a bus from the Haywards Heath station, a one-way journey could take over an hour if the connection was not right.

I would visit Terry for an hour and then home again. He came home but was only there for a short while and then went back into hospital this time for palliative care, but at the time, we did not know what it meant. I encouraged Trevor to visit in the evening, but Terry could not hear us so we just sat there giving spiritual support.

A few days on one early morning I was out walking the boys (Max and Sam) in the local park, and we were just going down the footpath when right in front of me was a £5 note. I picked it up and as I did Terry came into my mind, and I could see him laughing. I smiled and felt a warm feeling in me like a hug, and I knew he had gone. I rushed back home without walking the boys to let Trevor know, and he thought I was mad.

I had to insist several times before he eventually rang the hospital for news, and he was told that Terry had passed away half an hour previous. I was right, but Trevor had not wanted to listen to me (Just like my flipping Dad). I believe Terry came to me because I had been the only one to visit him regularly, and I had tried to cheer him up on my visits.

Before Terry passed away Trevor had been approached by a Company in London asking him to run a project they had on a salubrious Island in the Caribbean Mustique, but Trevor would not go as he did not want to be away from home if anything happened to Terry.

I was so surprised when after Terry's funeral which Jean and Luke had organised; Trevor took up the offer of working abroad because the position still had not been filled. Trevor was a meat and two veg plain home-cooked English meals chap and disliked any foreign food, but like some of his family, he liked the idea of rubbing shoulders with the rich and famous and being part of the expat group living permanently on the island this appealed to him greatly.

The arrangement with the company employing Trevor was that Trevor would work for six weeks and come home for one, and in those six weeks, Trevor and I would communicate by fax, so he got news from home regularly even the low down on how I'd managed to fix a plumbing issue I'd had and lived to tell the tale when my oven door glass blew up on me. I had leant down to open the door and the outer glass on the door blew towards me but landed in a straight line at my feet.

I can guarantee that my Guardian Angel was standing between me and the oven door. As I looked down there was a line of glass chippings right in front of me and none of it had touched me. I looked to the heavens and thanked them for protecting me.

I was trying to run a small business in the mini market in Town on Thursdays, Fridays and Saturdays, Steven was in Wales at University, and I was sending him food parcels. Trevor was in the Caribbean working and Alice had just passed her driving test and was buying herself a car. The boys and I were home with Alice trying to keep the home fires burning.

Yes, Trevor's time away was a lonely time for me and the boys, soon it was time for Steven to be starting his last year at University and Alice was now living away from home. Alice had contemplated University but not being an academic like her brother decided to leave school without going onto further education and got a job. Then she found herself a boyfriend, and within a few months, they bought a house together a few miles away, she was only nineteen.

I think in all honesty she wanted to prove to herself that if her brother could do university and fend for himself she could be all grown up and get a house with her boyfriend. They did get engaged, but it did not work out, and a year later, they split up and Alice moved back home.

Whilst everyone was away I had no transport and the routine with the boys was what kept me sane as visiting my parents was definitely out of the question. Trevor's family blamed me for his working abroad and did not visit once or ring me to see how I was coping the whole time Trevor was away. What they would not understand was that Trevor had no option at the time and working abroad was the only offer of work he'd had.

In the week that he came home Trevor just wanted to relax and he did bring me back perfume, and on a couple of occasions, the gardener on the estate gave Trevor flowers from the gardens to bring home. The only distinctive flower I remember was the Bird of Paradise. Food-wise, he was coping quite well and was not as picky as he was at home.

It was one of Steven's term breaks, and I had told him that I would cook his favourite meal—a roast dinner. He was so looking forward to it, and I was too just to have his company really. I chose to use chicken breast fillet in breadcrumbs with all the trimmings and lashings of vegetable gravy (This was something I used instead of red meat very often). As we were sitting down and talking about his university friends, Steven asked what meat had I chosen for dinner, and I told him, "the chicken in breadcrumbs."

"I don't think so," says he, and as I tasted it, I had used cod fillet in breadcrumbs. I was beside myself whereas Steven was rolling about with laughter and said that this story would go down really well with his mates when he got back. Steven ate all of his meal, but I just could not look at the fish in lashings of gravy but ate all my vegetables.

In his last year at University Steven had got engaged to his lovely girlfriend Nicola. She managed to switch universities to be with Steven in their last year at University. Plans were made when they got home and a year later with

Alice as one of the bridesmaids Steven and Nicola got married. Trevor had re-scheduled his week home to coincide with the wedding.

At the last minute, my dad acted the show off and spoiler and refused to go to the reception and that stopped Mum from attending. Mum was so upset and embarrassed as she was so looking forward to it. I too was angry and embarrassed and had to lie and make a convincing excuse on their behalf to Steven and Nicola's family.

My dad always did what he wanted and to hell with anyone's feelings. Jean had been invited, but she refused to attend although Luke and his girlfriend Rose came to give family support.

After the wedding and looking at the photos, I had asked Dad why he had kept his cap on for the photos, and he replied that he was doing his own thing and didn't want to be part of the 'show'. Mum and I could not understand why he had been so stroppy and hurtful. Steven was a bit put out as Nicola's family came out in force and quite rightly so. Another wedding Dad had to mess up and spoil.

As Alice's engagement had not worked out she came back home while they sold the house. Trevor was in the final stages of the building project on the island. He had loved his time there being treated like a lord by the locals and rubbing shoulders with the A list celebrities.

With Terry gone Jean was getting more possessive with Trevor, the other reason being that Luke wanted his girlfriend Rose to move into the house with him and Jean. After all, Luke still lived at home and shared all the bills with Jean. I know what Jean really wanted, it was to come and live with us now we had a spare bedroom. I had one bully in the house, and I was not about to have another.

Jean was not happy and refused to agree to have Rose move in and did not make life easy for them both. Jean reminded me so much of my grandmother who had disliked the women around her boys.

Rose lived in the same village and within a year of them knowing each other Rose was pregnant and Luke insisted Rose move in with them. Melany was born shortly after and life at home for Jean had got worse; personally, I think they were all as bad as each other. Jean was slowly being pushed to one side plus her sister had not long passed away after a massive stroke, and she did not get on with her brother-in-law so she was now quite isolated.

While everyone was away here there and everywhere, I still managed to run the business in the market selling all types of celebration items including making wedding posies, cakes and gifts. I also had a part-time evening job with Air Miles typing up air tickets at their offices across the road from home from 6:00 to 9:00 pm. I'd had these jobs before everyone had decided to go in different directions. I walked the boys three times a day for an hour each time and ran the home too.

Luckily, by this time also, the secondary school playing field at the back of us had been sold off to a supermarket chain, and they soon opened a big store on our doorstep. Not having a car to drive for the weekly shop, I had started going out through the back gate and across the road to get my shopping. The boys and I would also go out that way for the walks and it made sense on wet days too, as I was able to dry them in the conservatory before allowing them indoors.

Oh yes, the conservatory, I haven't told you how we got it, no we hadn't won the lottery it was a gift from the heavens. On one of the times that Trevor was made redundant, the company unexpectedly offered Trevor the option of cashing in the pension payments he had made and knowing that at the time, money would be tight again whilst he was looking for work, he took the money. It was a few thousand, but thankfully, he got his next job within a few weeks, and we decided that there had been a reason for us getting that money so we decided to have something lasting and beneficial for all of us—the conservatory. It paid for itself time and time again, as we would have all types of family gatherings and when I was at work I would leave the doors open slightly for the boys to go out into the garden and do what they needed to do.

When Alice came back home and working locally I asked for her to contribute to the household budget, but she was also starting to take things for granted, and I was doing her washing, ironing cooking, and I felt like a maid, like Trevor she was not contributing other than financially. I kept this going for over a year, and in the end, I could not take it any more as by now I had a part-time job as a cashier at the bank, and I never seemed to get a break. I gave Alice an ultimatum and said that if she did not help at home she would need to find a place of her own and Trevor, and I would help her with the deposit.

She already had funds from the sale of the property she had sold. When she got herself straight she could repay us. She agreed and soon found a ground floor flat in another part of Crawley. We helped as much as we could, but she had to learn for herself too.

She had already gone down the house ownership business before so it was not all that new for her, and we still gave her the chance to make her own choices. After all, she was now nearly twenty-two and an adult and had to learn responsibilities. We were close by and ready to help at any time.

Steven and Nicola first lived in rented accommodation in Caterham Surrey and would visit us now and then. Not long after they had moved to Caterham they had been making their way home from Crawley with a load of possessions in the car and were sideswiped by a foreign lorry. It was dark and must have seemed so frightening. Thank God they were both ok. Steven had rung home to tell us and Trevor went to see them and pick them up.

I had to stay home because the boys would have been on their own and as I was not sure how long we would be I did not think it was a good idea my going with Trevor. Unfortunately, this did not go down well with Nicola, and I was made to regret my decision not to go many times over. Just over a year on from that awful event, they found a lovely two-bed semi not far from us. We had managed to help them move into their home in Caterham along with Nicola's parents.

This time, I was really worried that Trevor could injure himself and not be able to work. We explained our concerns to Steven, and he seemed ok about it. Within weeks, Nicola was pregnant, and we were strongly encouraged to help them with stripping the walls and help with other bits. I was unhappy as we seemed to get all the messy jobs and also Trevor was doing this in his week home from the Island.

Eventually, the building project on Mustique finished and Trevor came home and Nicola gave birth to a gorgeous little girl named Melisa. Nicola's parents managed to buy a house a stone's throw away from Steven and Nicola so they could be close by and this was a few minutes from where we lived. We all shopped in the same supermarket, but I realised very soon that when I would catch sight of Nicola's parents in the supermarket, and I would go to greet them, in the blink of an eye they were gone. This happened so many times I got the impression that they were not keen on us meeting, but I never mentioned it to Steven.

I'd had so much grief from our parents on both sides in our married life that I was not going to make trouble for my children no matter what happened. For some reason, things did not gel with us all, and we were grandparents in name but did not get the chance to take part in Melisa's growing up. For a little while though I was allowed to collect Melisa from nursery when I finished work and bring her home and wait until Nicola came home. I got too friendly and played a lot with Melisa and I'd got the instinct impression that was wrong.

I remember once I was standing at the bus stop waiting to go back to work in the town centre and Steven's mother-in-law was coming towards me pushing Melisa in the open-top pushchair and bless her, little one spots me and calls out Nanny and points. Not a flicker or turn of the head from her Grandma, Lucy would have seen me no doubt about it. I just waved, smiled and blew Melisa a kiss and a big smile came across her face.

From then on I knew that Trevor, and I were not going to be accepted in the fold. As I said I only helped out for a few weeks, I got too close and friendly and it obviously was not what Steven and his family wanted. What was sad was that they were denying their child both sets of grandparents.

I could not understand why Nicola's parents were like that, they had three children and Melisa was their second grandchild. They knew we would not be able to have any Grandchildren from Alice as she had a condition that made it very difficult for her to have any, so I felt we needed to make the most of the children Steven would have. At the end of the day, it was not meant to be.

The universe had other plans for us. Don't for one minute think we did not care and feel really hurt because it did hurt an awful lot, and I would cry on many occasions and wonder why things had turned out that way.

Before I go any further I need to tell you about my car and how it helped me help those around me, the car had come from the heavens. It was a couple of years before the millennium, and I was working with a large stationery/newspaper retailer in the shopping precinct in Crawley I was getting a wage, and within a few months, I went to the local Ford dealer to buy a second-hand car. I was sold a triumph herald and within a week the something shaft went and I could not use it for some time because the garage had to repair it.

I'd been very angry as this car would be my passport to see my parents and also to help Jean now she was living not so far away and lonely. I told the dealer that if I did not get a reliable courtesy car I would go to Esther Rantzen (a programme on the TV fighting for the consumer). They offered me the Rover 25 that had been sitting on the forecourt, and I took it.

As time went on, the car was not repaired, and I confronted the dealer again threatening to go to the office of Fair Trading, Advertising Standards and anyone else who would listen. They told me that there were no vehicles for me to exchange my broken down one with. My original car could not be repaired, and I would have to choose another adding more costs to the original price of the first car.

So I told them that in that case, I wanted the Rover I had been driving for the past few weeks and at no extra cost. They went off scratching their heads; eventually, they gave in, and the documents were changed, and the Rover was mine. Woohoo result!

Cars to me are something that gets you from A to B it has four wheels, an engine and a steering wheel end of the story. Those who knew me and neighbours were wondering how I had managed to afford a Rover 25 and they made me feel that I had to justify my ownership of the Universe's gift. The reason the first car was not suitable was because unbeknown to me I had to have a more reliable one. The Rover was a gift because I wanted it to be able to help others in the family and to give me the chance to make their lives a bit better. That's when the Universe helps out. I have learnt that now, but I did not know it at the time.

You know when things keep happening to you and you long for a break? You're desperate for some time for yourself so that you can take stock, re-charge your batteries and take a deep breath and appreciate what you have. Well, I had been longing for that time and thought it was just around the corner, nope not a chance.

As the festivities of the millennium were being screened on the TV I wondered what the next ten years would hold for me. I was remembering back when I was a small child and I'd hear people talking about the year 2000; it would fill me with doom and gloom and dread of those years to come. I was really apprehensive about the future. My gut feeling was right and my apprehension was on the money.

I would be losing most of those close to me. The first ten years were to be the worse and most challenging and traumatic of my life. The only two beautiful things to happen in that decade were the birth of our granddaughter Hillary and our daughter Alice getting married to Darren.

In January 2000, my brother-in-law Luke decided to register Jean for the local sheltered housing block in the village, without any of the family being made aware. When we were told Jean was on the waiting list and could move at any time, the rest of the family thought it was with Jean's consent, but it was not. Luke and Rose had managed to carry out a few things behind everyone's backs and these eventually came out in legal proceedings a few years later.

In February 2000, my parents were at home watching television in their upstairs flat when someone came into the house downstairs and walked up to their open staircase and into their bedroom and took all their jewellery and money. Mum only realised what had happened when she went to get ready for bed. She was beside herself, and Dad was saying what he would have done had he heard them. Yeh! Yeh! I thought.

My uncles had since passed away and new tenants lived in the flat below. Mum was making herself so ill about this that I decided to start badgering the local council to help me transfer them down to where we lived in Crawley West Sussex. Thankfully with having the car I could carry out as many visits in taking Mum and Dad to the Council for interviews and paper shuffling.

I had even compiled a letter with photos of how the layout of their flat was and took notes of the temperatures they were enduring in the winter. I even made a video of how unsafe the flat was for people their age and what health issues they both had.

In the meantime, Luke was making arrangements for moving dates for Jean to move to a sheltered housing flat. Trying to keep a part-time job, running the home and looking after the boys and also helping Mum and Dad were no mean feat. By spring 2001, moving date for Jean came, and I organised a removal company and helped her with packing (everyone else had full-time jobs, Jean needed support).

My sister-in-law Lynda came down full of wow because she was expected to take time off work for the day, and like a little gremlin on your shoulder, she was stirring trouble about Luke and Rose. Like most good stirrers when the shit hits the fan they are blameless and clueless.

Trevor and Luke and Lynda's husband Jeff in the meantime carpeted the flat. The following day the removal chaps moved Jean into her new home.

Three weeks later, I was helping my mum and dad move out of their London home of forty years. I had driven up to London to make sure everything was taken and my youngest brother Albert had come up from Kent to help out too. He drove Mum and Dad down, and I took the remainder of the items, mainly the plants in my car. It had been decided that Mum and Dad would be better off coming down near me.

This relieved Albert as he could not see how things would work out with Mum and Dad moving to Kent. My dad was not pleased because he wanted one of the boys to be there for them, and they weren't. My brother Louis a few years earlier had moved to the Alps in France after having helped himself to all the possessions my uncles and Nan had left behind when they passed. He wanted my parents to move near him, but Mum and Dad would not agree and this angered him a great deal.

Eventually Mum and Dad settled in a council ground floor flat in Broadfield Crawley just seven miles from me and it would be easy to see them on a daily basis. They soon learnt the bus times which stopped just outside the flats in both directions. The shopping precinct was just across the road along with the surgery and Mum's favourite take away the Chinese food place. Mum thought she had died and gone to heaven. Dad on the other hand was not happy.

On the ground floor, he felt more vulnerable. The central heating made him too hot. They were now living close enough to me for me to notice how bullish Dad was. Poor Mum had put up for many years temperatures of around fifteen degrees in the winter, and she never once complained. There was also a scheme manager who would call them every morning on an intercom system in the flats, and she would make sure there were no problems.

Dad's moaning and arguments had made Mum so ill that just before her eightieth Birthday she had a massive heart attack, and we were not sure if she would pull through. I had to give in my notice at work as a cashier for a major bank, and I loved it. I felt I had achieved something when I went from retail into banking, and I was so proud of myself if no one else was.

My dad did not want to leave Mum, he was losing control, but I convinced him that it was for the best. I decided that so as not to upset everyone's routine at home i.e. Trevor that I should go and sleep at Mum and Dad's so that Dad had his routine and would be less troublesome. I would sleep on the settee. Then once he was ready and dressed I would drive us to my house walk and feed the boys then get all the jobs done.

After a couple of weeks, this was the routine along with visiting Mum twice a day. Mum was getting better. She was then ready to come home, but I had to keep an eye on them because I knew by then what a bully Dad really was. He would not have it that Mum was not to eat McDonald's food or such stuff.

He wanted Mum to eat the same dinners as him even the meals she would cook at home. There were constant arguments between them, and Dad was not happy that I was on hand so much. I remember him saying to Mum, "Who would have thought it, that it would be the girl?" When I heard him say that I asked Mum what he meant she said that he had always thought one of the boys would look after us, but Dad never imagined it would be you. That hurt, but it did not stop me from helping both of them.

Mum was doing quite well, and since her coming home from the hospital, I was taking them shopping and doing all the heavy lifting. After a few weeks of Jean moving into her sheltered flat, I would once a week go down and visit. I would take the boys with me as she loved seeing them. Then I realised she was not going out very often so once a week I would go down to see her and take her out for a cuppa and a cake or shopping.

She would say how she appreciated my efforts. She loved just sitting, people watching. I would have to coax Trevor to visit his mum at times as he would think well she had already had a visit from me why should he have to go. At times I would let him go on his own with the boys.

My mum had her eightieth Birthday in spring 2002, and by the end of that year, she was ill again with her heart and diabetes. I explained to the surgery and the hospital that the demands from my dad and his bullying was too much for Mum, and they wanted to put Dad in a home, and we looked around, but it never got any further.

Then one day Mum came home from another stay in hospital this time about her diabetes, and Dad started having a go at her about me interfering all the time and Mum retaliated. Next thing she knows he has put his coat on and gone out. It was a while later that Mum called me, it was around 4:00 pm, and she told me what had happened. I left a note for Trevor for when he got home and got in the car and drove down the 7 miles.

I got there thinking Mum would be beside herself, and she wasn't. She was angry at him for acting like a child and always wanting his own way. She was so fed up that she wished he would not come home. I ran up to the shops looking in all of them, asking shopkeepers if they had seen him. I even went up to the bus stops at the end of the parade but nothing.

I went back to Mums and phoned the police informing them that Dad may be confused. Confused, my foot, he had gone straight to the bus stop got on a bus and walked straight into McDonald's and chatted with the staff, who advised him to go home as we may be looking for him. An hour later, he walked in as bold as brass without a thought for any of us. I could swear that he had enjoyed his freedom and was smiling to himself. I informed the police that he had returned home and all was well.

I could see things were getting worse, and I knew that I had to keep a closer eye on them both from now on. I would make up all their pillboxes for the week, re-order any medication, put the prescription into the surgery. Also because of her diabetes, Mum had to visit the nurse once a week to have her feet dressings changed. Dad took a lot of convincing for me to do this as I was taking charge of more of his tasks.

The trouble was his walking was very poor, he could not explain what health issues Mum had and would argue the toss with me and the doctor as to what problems Mum was having at home. Although Dad was not able to tell the doctor what was going on with Mum he still had to be present and at times would make comments that were not relevant.

Whilst I was going through all the dramas with my parents I had still been visiting Jean at the sheltered housing. I'd had her medication locked up as she would forget that she had taken her pills and take another dose and when she got one of her 'muzzy heads' as she called them she would take paracetamol like sweets and without any water. Her dementia was getting worse and taking her to the local GP surgery was very hard. I would have to lie that we were going out and take her via the surgery on the premise that I was picking up her prescription.

The staff knew what she was like and would just gesture for us to go ahead and see the doctor. That's when she would start accusing me of all sorts. We'd enter the doctor's office, and she would shout and tell him that I had lied to her, there was nothing wrong with her, and she would argue non-stop. The doctor would always tell her that she was being unkind to me and that she was lucky to have someone so caring thinking of her.

We had all been given some lovely news; Steven and Nicola were expecting another baby. Within weeks, Mum was back in the hospital with more heart problems and this time as Dad's dementia was getting worse and for the sake of my sanity, I decided to have him move into our house at night-times. It was such a mistake, he would get up in the night and not realise where he was, I slept so lightly that I was up within seconds fearing he would fall down the stairs.

I persevered for a while longer, I made an appointment for Dad to see the GP so that he could confirm Dad's state of mind, but Dad was so nice and cooperative I was made to look as though I was making it all up. Going to visit Mum in hospital he would argue with me, saying that Mum should be home with him, why was I getting involved as he was capable of looking after her. It just went on and on, and on many occasions, it was taking me back to my days at home and my having to walk on eggshells, and I couldn't believe it because I was doing just that all over again.

He would start arguing with me and then hurry himself out into the garden. At one time I would have gone out to placate him and cowl down but no more. I just carried on ironing and getting angrier about the situation he was placing me in. It took him a while, but he came in and sat down contemplating. He was scheming something and that bothered me.

On this particular day, we had got out of the car and were walking towards the entrance of the hospital to visit Mum.

Dad had been given a walking stick to use for his back as he was beginning to walk with a stoop; he didn't want the stick and was dragging it behind him all the time and nearly tripping people up. In the end, he gave it to me to carry to stop me from moaning at him to use it properly.

As we approached the main doors to the hospital he turned to me and said, "I don't know who they think they are in here, but your mum is coming home." Oh God, I thought as it sent a shiver down my back. We got into the six-bed ward, and he spotted her, greeting Mum with smiles and a kiss, but I could hear it in his voice, it was the same tone he would have when there was going to be trouble.

Mum bless her was looking so well, being in there without worrying about him I was not surprised, and I was so chuffed that she could make herself understood and at times there would be a nurse who would speak French, and she was glad of that. She just could not believe how nice the staff were and how much patience they had. Of course, she had only ever frequented family and most of the time that would be Dad. She had been given a taste of life outside her confines of home and was relishing it.

We sat and chatted whilst Dad was pensive and stern with Mum, she asked him what the matter was (I remember thinking—no don't ask you will trigger him off).

That was it, in French, of course, he accused her of lingering in hospital whilst he had to struggle at home alone, there was nothing wrong with her and that she should come home now and proceeded to pull her out of the bed. What had incensed him so much was that he could see the staff laughing and joking with her and the more it happened the more he was enraged.

He became so abusive and loud that I called a member of staff and explained the situation, and they asked him to move to the office. Mum was so upset, I calmed her down and went out to speak to the staff and said this is what she will be going home to and drew a rough picture of life at home for Mum. I asked if he could be taken to a rest bite ward but that was not possible; the only way would be to have him sectioned under the mental health act, but Mum would have to sign the papers.

Oh dear God, things were escalating so fast and their priority was Mum's well-being, he was so out of it with rage, anger and frustration at not getting his own way it scared me as I had never seen him this bad.

Eventually, Mum signed the papers, and he was taken to a unit at a small cottage hospital seven miles away in Horsham. I could not visit Dad for twenty-four hours. Now I would have two hospital visits to make, I contacted my youngest brother Albert and explained everything. He felt it was wrong for Dad to be sectioned so I turned to him and said, "It's about time you visited them and saw how things were for yourself."

The next day, he went to the mental health unit to visit Dad but only got as far as the ward door and did U-turn. I was spitting chips as there was another one of 'their boys' not helping or giving me support, after that episode I knew I was on my own.

When I was finally allowed to visit Dad he was calm and could not understand where he was. He was like a fish out of water he could not understand why he was with 'these' people and asked for Mum.

After explaining to him that it was a temporary measure and that they would both be home together again, he calmed down. The conversations consisted of questions and answers going round and round in circles. Dad had obviously been given medication to calm him down and that was how I had managed to speak to him calmly.

As I was driving back home to some peace and quiet I prayed that God would give me the strength and stamina to look after both of them and that I could still be able to run my home and look after my boys as there was nobody else to take some of the pressure. I was scared as I was not sleeping well, and I was getting severe panic attacks at night which Trevor was at times not happy about because I was waking him up in a blind panic believing I was going to die, and I needed him to reassure me that I would be alright. There were only ever groans and in the morning he would not be happy at having had broken sleep.

The upshot of the whole fiasco was that Dad would have to stay in the unit for Mum's sake and that Social Services would be in touch so that we could visit care homes and choose a suitable transfer from the unit. Mum by this time had come home from the hospital and was sent home. To give her some time to get used to her new life and routine, she decided that visiting her once a day was enough, and I would still make up her medication and take her to the nurse etc., but we had to think about what the long term plan would be.

After a few days of being on her own, Mum decided to come with me to visit Dad. She was apprehensive but at least she was not alone. We arrived and signed in, opened the doors to the ward and walked down the long corridor that was lined on the right-hand side with cubicle rooms for each patient. Then turning left you walked into a large open plan room with a kitchen and office at the far end.

The hall was filled with tables and chairs and about halfway down was my dad, a pitiful figure sitting at a table and looking into his hands (I must tell you this was one of the most emotional moments in my life, my dad had always been a strong proud dominant figure in my life. A person never to be messed with and now he was reduced to this). It was so painful, I just wanted him back home and him being nice to Mum, but I knew that would no longer be possible and life for all of us would never be the same again.

Mum was more shocked than I and as we sat down his face lit up, and he spoke to us in a manner that he believed my mum was his mum and that I was Albert. He never mentioned Mum or me at all. Mum was so hurt and could not understand why he was thinking in that way. I left her with Dad and asked to speak to the consultant.

He explained that Dad had been put on medication to calm him down as when he came in he was very abusive to the staff and patients. This was now a week later, and I asked for some medication to be taken away. This they did, but unfortunately, the one they kept him on had bad side effects and was even mentioned in the national paper a few weeks later.

It was a hot Sunday afternoon, and Mum and I were going to visit Dad and Trevor decided to come along—I nearly fell over backwards.

I had managed to shelter Trevor from most of the goings-on, and his life had been virtually unchanged. When we arrived Dad was sitting in one of the armchairs, and we ushered him to one of the tables. He recognised Trevor but still thought of Mum and I were other members of the family.

Dad said he wanted to use the toilet, and he went, and he was in sight of us all. We sat talking and as time went on Dad was taking some time so I asked Trevor to go and see. Trevor called me to get a member of staff as Dad had fallen off the toilet and grazed his knee and Trevor could not manage to lift Dad off the floor.

There were no qualified members of staff the staff present could not find the plasters. One had to go to the main hospital building and get some from them.

On the following day, I visited Dad and asked to speak to the Nurse in charge and the Doctor. I explained what had happened the previous day, and they were not apologetic but said they would investigate. I visited Dad every day from the first day he was admitted, I owed it to him. He and Mum had given up so much to bring us all to England for a better life and it did not matter how awful my upbringing was he still deserved my respect and care no matter what.

Around three weeks after his accident in the toilet Mum was back in the hospital due to her failing heart and diabetes. The Doctor at the hospital asked to speak with me and informed me that Mum's condition was so much in the balance that they only predicted she would be with us for only about six months. I rang and told my brother Albert the news and he immediately came to visit with his wife Carol and adopted daughter, Suzie. This immediately got Mum wondering why the visit; it was out of character, and his excuse was that they were going to visit Dad at the other hospital unit too.

Due to the way my dad had ruled my mum's life for over fifty years, she would never be able to go into a home, even though I would never consider it. She could only speak French and a bit of English. I chatted with Trevor and explained that Mum would need to come and live with us. We needed to go for a bungalow large enough for Mum to have her own lounge and bedroom.

With this discussion still ringing in my ears and scrabbling around in my brain I visited Dad. It was late afternoon and the visit went quite well, better than I had hoped. Dad decided to go and sit by the main doors on one of the armchairs next to another patient. According to the staff, Dad was quite protective of this other gentleman, but they made a bad joke about it, implying that Dad fancied this chap.

I laughed with the staff and thought that this insinuation would have enraged Dad so much that he would kill anyone thinking that about him. The staff moved away, and I kissed Dad goodbye as always, and as I was leaning towards him, he said, "You wait and see. I'll show you, you wait and see," and waved me away to go home. Dad's voice was so menacing it sent a shiver down my back, and I thought what plan would he be hatching now.

The one thing that I hated more than anything was walking out and leaving him behind. On many occasions, he'd followed me and would call for me to wait for him as he wanted to come home with me, it would break my heart hearing him calling and shuffling behind me trying to catch me up. Sometimes I would have to walk back and ask the staff to occupy Dad whilst I went out.

At the same time, as all this was going on, Steven gave us the news that little Hilary had come into this world. I was so pleased to have managed a visit the day after she was born in Redhill Hospital, and I even had the pleasure of changing her nappy. I was so nervous but happy at being able to do something for my new Granddaughter as I had never been given the chance to do this with Melisa.

Nicola mentioned a few days later that she had given me the task knowing that the nappy would be a horrid one and thought I should have the pleasure of cleaning Hilary up. Not very nice of you I thought, but I still got to change her nappy woohoo.

On my visit to see Dad the following day, which I was not looking forward to because of his attitude the night before, I got in through the doors and walked round to the main lounge, and I could not see him. I asked the staff, and they said he was sleeping in his bed and had not wanted to get up. I thought it was odd and when I went into the room, it was in full darkness and a really odd thing he was sleeping on his back with his knees up. He never slept like that ever.

I approached him to kiss him and knew straight away there was something wrong. His breathing was very shallow, and he was cold to the touch, and he would not wake. I quickly called for a Doctor, and they had to ring for one from the main building. The Doctor asked for me to wait in the lounge and immediately she came back to say Dad was in a coma, and she was transferring him to the main building for closer examination and care. The trolley came, and he was put on it, the Doctor, another member of staff, and I ran through the car park rushing Dad into the main Hospital through the emergency doors at the back and into the closest side room.

I waited for what seemed ages and the Doctor told me that Dad had a massive stroke and was now in a coma, and she would do everything she could to make him comfortable, and we could visit at any time. I knew dam well what had happened, he had been so angry at the comments from the staff the night before that he must have refused to go to bed, and they had left him to his own devices. He had the massive stroke in the night sitting in the armchair and in the morning they realised what had probably happened and put him in bed, but his knees were still up as he would have been in the sitting position when he went into the coma. I could have bet my life on it.

This incident reminded me of when Mum and Dad had moved into their ground floor flat in Broadfield and Dad turned to me pointing to the chair in the lounge by the kitchen door and said, "See this chair that is where I am going to die." I looked at Dad thinking why are you saying that? In the unit where he'd had his stroke and went into the coma, the armchair was next to the doors leading to the corridor to all the rooms. He knew two years before he died.

The Doctor taking charge would have had to do something to have him lying flat so the family could visit and not be upset. He was given the last rights and a week after his hurried entry to the main hospital Dad passed away. I instinctively knew when Dad had passed away. I rang the hospital for news at around 5:00 am, and they told me that Dad had passed away a few minutes before my call.

Later that morning, I went to see Mum and tell her the news, we both broke down crying, I think mostly from relief at no more bullying, then sadness at the way things had unfolded over the last few months and that things were going to change again for both of us.

I would have had every right to fight the hospital for the way my dad had been treated but with having to look after Mum now and the fact that she too would be leaving us soon, I chose not to take it any further. Whether I did the right thing I shall never know.

The first thing I did for both of us was to take us to Pizza Hut for lunch. We were both so looking forward to it as Dad would never agree because he would make such a fuss and commotion that it put us off going there.

We sat at the table next to each other and all of a sudden we started laughing and laughing and we could not stop for a few minutes. Both of us welling up with emotion and then crying. I wanted to hug and kiss Mum and tell her everything was going to be alright, but there were too many people around us. I just grabbed her hand and squeezed it.

I remember the meal came, and we were talking about Dad and men in general, and she let slip that being sexually abused by your husband was acceptable and their right. Well, I just flew into a rage and said to her that it was not and should never be accepted as such; unfortunately, some of the anger I showed was because I could relate to her beliefs, but I could not tell her why. It was something I would have to keep to myself. Mum had got upset at my reaction, and I apologised, and we carried on chatting and eating our meal enjoying every morsel.

Mum and I made the funeral arrangements, but the funeral directors were in South London, and we both went there for the payments and everything else that had to be decided. They would collect Dad from the hospital mortuary the following day. Alice and I had the chance to visit Dad at the hospital mortuary before the funeral directors came. I told Alice she should not come in, but she wanted and it was the wrong thing for her to do as she was so upset and sobbing that she had to go out quite quickly.

My dad had wanted my brother Louis to be notified when he died. I had to contact my brother Louis in France, and I was not looking forward to it. I heard a voice in French and asked if it was Lora Louis' wife. She confirmed in French and passed me over to Louis, he was very hostile, and he reminded me of Dad. I explained about Dad and the funeral date and time, and he said he would try and attend and hung up.

On the day of the funeral, I asked to visit Dad to say goodbye. Nobody else wanted to come with me. It was not something I was looking forward to, but it had to be done. When the time came the coffin had been placed up high above another one, and I had to go on tiptoes to see his body, I was half expecting him to lean over and grab me and say what have you done to me in a loud and angry voice, but he never, it was final Dad was being buried that day.

The funeral date had been the same date in September that my grandmother had died which I found really uncanny as they both loved each other so much.

As we gathered for Dad's funeral service I suddenly caught sight of Louis with his daughter Jilly. He went straight to Mum and cuddled her and was upset. As he got up he turned towards me, and I said, "It's nice to see you both."

But I did not get that far I only managed half of the sentence, and he grabbed my blouse tight around my neck and his face came into mine and said in a menacing way, "If you ever speak to me again, I will cut your throat."

"Well, ok," I replied if that is how you feel. If Albert had been present he would have floored him, Trevor stood next to me and did nothing per usual.

As Louis let go of me he turned to Trevor and greeted him and Trevor returned the greeting, as though nothing had just taken place. I was dumbstruck. (It reminded me of a time when we lived in Larkfield and one of the neighbours had come round and was banging on our front door wanting to smack my face and do all sorts of things because she had heard from another neighbour I had said this that and the other.

I was firstly shocked at her attitude and my being accused of something I had not said but more so at Trevor's attitude, he invited her in for a coffee. I was so annoyed at him and upset I left them both and went upstairs until she had left.)

Trevor and I had thought we should have a break, and Mum thought it would be a good idea too. After the funeral, we had a week in a cottage in Cornwall. It was a nice week away, but I think it may have been a bit too much for Mum. On our return, we started looking for a new home for all of us.

In the meantime, Alice was quite settled in her ground floor flat and more pleased that her granddad had been able to visit her at home. She'd decided she wanted someone to share her life with and went on the internet. She had spoken to some really strange blokes and it worried me silly. She eventually met this chap, and they decided to meet in Brighton. I was so nervous, but he turned out to be a lovely young man.

Alice would not tell me what he looked like or anything about him, but I kept an open mind. When they came to see us for the first time, I opened the door and gave them a big smile and hello. Alice was disappointed as she had expected me to give him an odd look and be surprised and disapproving. Darren had a number one haircut and piercings on his face.

A few months later, they had decided to get engaged, and we had a big gathering at a Harvester. Jean was invited, Steven and his family Alice and her fella Darren and of course Trevor mum and I. Sitting at the large table having the meal I could not help having a few thoughts of Dad and how he would have moaned about the meal or the noise or something else.

We started looking at properties in earnest Trevor kept looking at big properties and was thinking beyond our means—per usual. Mum came with us as she should also have a say where she would be living.

After looking at quite a few properties, we revisited a large bungalow—yes, I said large, situated in the same town where Dad had passed away, Horsham. The bungalow was at the edge of the town with a large supermarket just over the dual carriageway and was situated right opposite a nature reserve. I knew that it would guarantee us having wildlife in the garden.

One problem was nobody would give us a mortgage because Trevor was the only one with the income. I wanted us to go for something smaller, but Trevor said we should keep trying other lenders. On one of my visits into town I was talking to one of my friends from the bank, and she suggested I should talk to the mortgage advisor at the far desk. I thought I can't lose anything.

To cut a long story short the bank was willing to give us a mortgage on the income from Trevor (three times his salary) my carer's allowance and my mum's pension credit. We were literally up against the wall, and I was really nervous, but Trevor was all gung-ho, and we signed on the dotted line.

Horsham West Sussex

The property sat on a third of an acre with a little stream to one side. There were four good sized bedrooms a huge lounge, a small office, a large dining area that had all these rooms leading off it. A large garage and a small angled separate room at the back of it, a large tiered patio at the back with grass and shrubs bordered by trees all around.

The front could accommodate up to three cars within the shrubs making the boundary and through the wide gate a grassed area to the pavement edge. All I kept thinking was I'd still got the boys to walk twice a day (they were getting old and needed less walking). I was also looking after Mum 24/7 and Trevor would be at work. All the cleaning and gardening involved really unnerved me. My gut instinct for this property was not favourable.

Before Mum could move in with us, the carpets had to be replaced and Trevor and the boys spent a couple of nights there before our furniture was moved in. Mum came in a week later, and she could not understand why she was not able to move in with us at the same time, and I thought you are joking me darling, who do you think I am Superwoman?

What did I say way back? "If it doesn't rain, it pours." Well, it came in bucket loads. The drains outside the property were blocked up because of all the shrubs and roots coming through the drains, which should have shown up when the survey was done before the purchase. Then Trevor lost his job a few months later and was desperate to find another, but by now, he was getting on in years and London was changing fast and the industry was more cut-throat than before. Not being that type of person he eventually found work down south and at a slower pace and much less money.

I tried to give Mum as much freedom and rest and relaxation as possible. I did all the cooking and housework and pretty much everything else, and Mum was responsible for her lovely large bedroom and her comfortable lounge with television and all her bits of furniture from her flat. She could go and sit anywhere in the bungalow and use any of the areas, but those two rooms were hers and entering her lounge or bedroom I would always knock on the opened door. It was my way of showing her respect, and of course, I was entering her private space.

Every day, we went out either for shopping or a light lunch and walkabout. After a while, Mum got fed up picking the place for us to visit so I got bits of paper and wrote different destinations on them folded them up and put them in a box. Each day at breakfast I would shake the box and get Mum to pick a piece of paper.

We're only talking of about a ten–twelve-mile radius, on the odd occasion it would stretch to twenty miles, but it had to be on one of her good days. Mum really loved visiting Cranleigh and Reigate in Surrey; someone once told me that Ringo Star lived in Cranleigh.

I did 90% of the decorating and the grass cutting which would take up to three hours each time. The boys loved the open space and sniffing out the foxes first thing in the morning they would come back indoors for breakfast with faces and legs dripping with the dew. Bats flew around the tall trees at night and at times we would have over twenty squirrels around the bird feeders.

On some days, we heard the Green Woodpecker and in the right season the Cuckoo. There was a deer farm not far from us and one had managed to come onto our land at the bottom and would appear every now and then. On those occasions, I would keep the boys inside or on a lead just in case.

I would feel sad for Jean sitting in her flat not wanting to take part in any activity the complex offered, and she never went anywhere. So at least once a month I would encourage Trevor to go and collect Jean from home and bring her over for the weekend.

Before Mum and Dad had moved down to Crawley, I would invite Jean a lot of the time when I was working in retail, she would meet me from work, and she would come and stay the weekend. Jean would always find ways to insult or hurt me. At lunch, she would say to Trevor, "We'll keep this one shall we?" He would then agree with her.

Or she would say, "Oh Trevor, come home to Mummy; come and live with me."

Trevor would never say no or disagree. This went on for a very long time, and in the end, I got really fed up to the back teeth—yes, I still had those and still do. I warned him that if Jean made those comments again, and he did not turn her down, his bags would be packed and in the car before he could blink and if he didn't believe me, to just try it.

It was his fault for giving her the wrong impression over the years that he was not enjoying married life, and he would pretend he was being hard done by and was downtrodden, and I would call him a liar and ask in front of his family why he was making me out to be the bad person. He would say nothing but grimaced.

My mum was enjoying life with us, and I was getting to know my mum, and about some of the relatives, I would never get to meet. It was hard to hide from Jean that my mum lived with us, but I'd like to think we managed it. I found it extremely hard to maintain the grounds by myself, and I tried to add borders to reduce the grass cutting. We had moved in at the end of 2004, and by the end of 2005, Mum's health had improved and was quite stable, even the hospital Consultant and GP were amazed and put it down to the care Mum was receiving from me.

The Rover needed servicing and one of the front wipers was playing up. I took it into the garage near home and was asked all the usual questions as I was a new customer to this particular garage. I mentioned my concerns about the wipers, and I was to collect the car at the end of the day.

When I returned I was a bit apprehensive because it was a ten-year-old car, but according to the mechanic/owner of the garage, it was in good nick and had obviously been well looked after according to the logbook. He asked me to walk to the car with him and as he sat in the driver's seat he said, "I thought you said there was no air con in the car."

"There isn't," I replied.

"What's this button for then?" He pointed to a button on the dashboard.

"NO WAY," I shouted. "I don't believe it, you are joking me. I have had the car all this time, and I have had the windows down to keep cool." He laughed so much at my reaction he could hardly get out of the car seat.

"I have told my mates in the pub about you not realising you had air con and it has been the best joke for a while, I even got asked if you were blond." How embarrassing at being the joke in the pub.

Alice and Darren got married towards the end of 2005 at a Hotel on the outskirts of Horsham and it was also handy when we needed to check up on the boys, Trevor offered to do that and it was only just once.

Alice had decided to ask our friend and hairdresser to help her get ready but had not told me, so when I went up to see if she was ok I found out that I was not needed, and I turned to go back down, as I would not have wanted to go against Alice's wishes. My friend said, "Don't go we can all do this." She had obviously felt awkward and did not want any bad feelings. There would not have been any on my part. Alice had to agree but was not pleased.

I had made the wedding cake and Darren's mum had made little knitted gifts to go around, and Trevor and I had paid for the reception. Alice decided not to invite Jean as she had refused to attend Steven's wedding. Oh, what a to-do weddings and funerals are.

It would not have bothered me if I had not helped Alice, she should have stuck to her decision. Getting dressed and ready was her choice for some reason, and I just wanted her to have her day filled with happiness.

After selling her flat and moving into rented accommodation with Darren, Alice realised that I would not take sides about Steven wanting to be with Nicola's parents more than with us. She could not understand that it was his choice, and I would not have an argument with him about it. Although it was very upsetting for all of us, I had to respect his wishes and I refused to upset the apple cart.

Alice decided to confront Steven about shunning us, and she was not happy that his life would no longer involve us as much as it had done. Steven said that his family was very important to him and his responsibilities were with them, and she should respect that.

A couple of months later, Alice and Darren found work for both of them up North near Manchester, and they moved quite soon after. My mum was so upset at firstly missing out on the great-grandchildren as Steven did not visit that often and now she was losing her granddaughter.

Bearing in mind that should anything happen to Mum Alice would never be able to just 'pop down'. Like I said before as parents we must trust that our children will do what is best for them. If their lives include us as parents, then we are very lucky and should enjoy every moment.

Trevor was beginning to get disenchanted with life at the cottage, I don't know why because he was only expected to go to work and bring his mum down for a visit every now and then. He should have changed places with me then he would have appreciated his job more. He was missing the buzz of London and the high profile jobs. He was also feeling jealous of the closeness Mum and I had got.

In July 2006, Mum and I had gone to one of the garden centres for tea and cake and within minutes of us being there the lights in the barn started flickering, then going off and coming back on. This went on for a few minutes, and I was getting more and more nervous because I knew in my heart that there was trouble at home with the boys (don't ask me how I knew, I just knew it, and I so desperately wanted to get home) but I could not make Mum believe me or understand the feeling I had. After half an hour, we made for home. I opened the front door and saw Max lying behind the door, he had died.

I just howled with sadness at not coming home earlier, Mum could not control me I could not stop crying and Sam just looked at me and cuddled up to me. The boys were by now sixteen years old (Twice the age the vet told me they would live for when he first saw them as puppies). I could not lift Max by myself but covered him with a blanket until Trevor got home, and we took him to the veterinarian hospital in East Grinstead fifteen miles away where they had always gone for treatment.

Sam had to come too, in order for him to see where we were leaving Max. They had both been to the hospital so many times. In the months that followed Sam came with us everywhere. He would search for Max, or on many occasions, he would stare at the front door.

Towards the end of 2006, Mum and I were at a crossroads controlled by traffic lights and as we were halfway across the road from the opposite direction came a car it turned right and straight into the side of my Rover. As I pulled to one side, I saw the other car had stopped further down the road I ran over to the driver, I looked inside and the woman driver told me she was eight months pregnant and had not seen me, then I saw in the back seat was a toddler no more than two years old.

My Rover was a right off, but I was given enough by the insurance company to put a deposit on a new Nissan Micra and the balance was paid on the credit card. Mum and I were OK but shocked.

Sam's mobility was getting worse, and eventually, the walks had become a crawl up the road. It was just after Christmas, and he sat looking up at me, and I knew he'd had enough. Don't ask how I knew, from very early on the boys, and I had our own thought language and nobody knew how we communicated, but we did very successfully. For sixteen years through all the goings-on with family and all the meals, I cooked for them every day we never stopped loving each other unconditionally.

The boys were born with a digestive disorder which meant that they had to have cooked plain food. Then after each meal, I would give them hide chews and a large Bonio biscuit. The vet had once said that for their age they had really healthy teeth, and I put that down to their diet and the chews after their meals. Their condition also meant that nobody would insure them.

At the end of December, I told Trevor it was cruel to keep Sam going, and we took him to the vet, and he agreed that Sam should be put to sleep, and Sam passed away in my arms. It was just as bad as when I had found Max. Fourteen years on, and I am still bawling my eyes out telling you about them, I still miss them so much. They were the closest I have ever got to being given so much love.

We were now in 2007, and Mum's health was a juggling act trying to keep all her conditions in balance with all the medication she was taking. Visits to the surgery were more frequent and the nurse visits for changing the dressings on Mum's feet were also more frequent.

One day I decided to look at what Mum was eating other than her home-cooked meals. There had to be something that was causing the soreness between her toes. After a couple of days and by a process of elimination, I discovered that it was the Diabetic sweets that Mum bought regularly. As they were hard to get hold of Mum would at times have to go without them for over a week some times.

It was at this time the sores would clear up. I kept a note of the situation, and we did discover that it was the sugar in the sweets, chocolates and other diabetic confectioneries that was making her feet bad. Mum very reluctantly stopped eating them, and she never had the problem come back.

In February 2007, on one weekend, we decided to try and go to Bluewater shopping centre in Kent as Mum had never been. We had left the M23 and turned onto the M25 towards Kent. We were going up the hill and in the middle lane. The lorry to my left was not giving any indication of coming out so I put my foot down and as I came alongside him he too was pulling out, having no chance to move out of its way the lorry nudged the Micra and the wheels were grinding into the side of the car where Trevor was in the front and Mum behind him.

The lorry driver pulled back in, and I pulled back too. It was really frightening and after a few miles and still waiting for him to pull out I decided to pass him, but again he came out at me. This time he came at such a force that he pushed the front of the Micra towards the central barrier we spun around two or three times, each time getting closer to the hard shoulder and the cars behind us were now pulling back or stopping. Eventually, we came to a standstill on the hard shoulder. I don't know how I got to it as I had taken my hands and feet of the controls when we had been hit.

Seeing all that traffic coming towards us as the car was spinning, I had thought that this was it; we would all be dead or in hospital. I had been really concerned for Mum as the shock on its own could kill her.

Drivers from behind could see all that happened and stopped to be witnesses. Others had called the emergency services and one driver noticed that in the far distance down the hill the lorry driver had stopped and was coming back. As he got to me I started shouting at him and asking if he was blind.

He smirked and said, "No speak English; I French."

I thought oh boy your day just got even worse. I shouted at him in French telling him my mother was so ill that she could have another heart attack, that he could have killed all of us. He was very apologetic and upset as he must have thought we were French too. To cut another long story short, Mum and I were taken by ambulance to the nearest hospital, Trevor was given a lift home by the breakdown lorry driver and then Trevor came to collect us in his car after Mum had been given the all-clear.

Trevor was told by the police attending the scene that around twenty-five incidents a week occurred on that stretch of the road involving foreign lorry drivers. Trevor was also advised not to bank on any response to a claim soon as some take a very long time. Within weeks of our contacting a solicitor with all the details and information and doctor's report, the compensation came through.

Trevor received over £1000 for his whiplash injuries, Mum received over £2000 due to her whiplash and knee injury, and I received £500 for injury to my lower back muscles.

The outcome to all this could have been far worse and one or all of us could have died. The fact that I had the presence of mind to take my hands and feet off the controls and letting fate take over saved us.

Had I not done that the impact and result of our injuries would have been quite different? I also believe that my speaking French to the driver made him think we were French and that admitting his guilt at the scene hurried things along. One thing Mum's compensation did do, it gave her the funds to put away for her funeral.

Having had the two car accidents five months apart Mum was very nervous about going out with me. I did keep reminding her that neither was my fault. I'd been given a courtesy car whilst mine was repaired. My Nissan was taken to a bodywork garage near home.

When my little Nissan Micra came back from the body shop you could not tell that she had been in an accident. Had my arms been long enough I would have hugged my little car. Oh yes, I never told you about Trevor's car. When I was in the process of buying my Micra to help those around me, Trevor had decided that he too would buy himself a car—a Jaguar.

He had always wanted one. What? I thought at the time that mine was to help, but his would be to show off as we did not need two cars and could not afford such a gas-guzzling car as he would also use it to go to work. I was so angry with him.

After the Motorway accident at the beginning of 2007, Trevor was made redundant by Jaguar on the south coast. He eventually found another job later on in the year near Seaford on the coast. I could tell the pressure on him with a large mortgage was getting him down, and he resented the life Mum and I were enjoying. A month after his redundancy Mum had a bad turn and he had become more frail. Her medication, and meals, walking, resting, everything was a balancing act.

For the past few years, I had been giving her the insulin injections she needed twice a day. As hard as I tried I just could not make things better, because that's what you do, isn't it? When you love someone and you care for them, your actions can have an impact on their well-being. This time I just could not do it on my own or with guidance from the GP so Mum was admitted at Redhill hospital nearly twenty-two miles away as this was the only place that had vacant beds.

Mum was in the hospital for ten days, and at first, I visited her twice a day then after a few days Mum could see it was taking up all my time to visit and the staff made her feel so comfortable Mum was happy for my once a day visit in the evening. At the same time, I would still visit Jean two or three times a week.

Due to her dementia, Jean had been transferred to a care home in East Grinstead. I would drive up from Horsham to visit Jean, took her out often as she did not like to mix with the residents. She was always waiting for family to call and take her out. On many occasions, I would have Mum in the car. We would collect Jean from the care home and go on to have lunch at a garden centre.

All you ever got from Jean was, "Look at all this expensive stuff. Who would want to buy it?"

My mum on the other hand did not have savings but enjoyed buying a little souvenir from wherever we went. Once a week I volunteered at Jean's care home to help them make cards for family and friends, I had found it thoroughly enjoyable and a good time was had by all of us. The trouble was Jean did not want to make things and objected to my doing anything for the residents. In her mind, I was there to visit her and not them.

After ten days, Mum came home and the stay in hospital this time had slowed her down considerably. I needed to help her shower as just brushing her teeth would tire her out. Mum found going out more tiring than before. The trouble was her being mobile was so important for her well-being.

The bungalow was large enough for her to walk around indoors. She did her own washing, ironing and dusting, but I drew a line at her hoovering and changing the bedding I was not happy with her doing the ironing either.

Mum would never have given up ironing because when she had left school as a very young girl, Mum trained to iron for a living and was brilliant at it. Dad's shirts would always come out of the draw as though they were new and just been brought out of their packaging. His trousers were ironed and pressed and looked new.

We would have heated discussions on many occasions about my inept way of ironing Trevor's shirts. She would take the garment from me and proceeded to show me the correct way of ironing a shirt. I could not understand why I had to follow her instructions as Trevor's shirts were always hung in the wardrobe, something Mum just could not abide by. Ho-hum!

It was on the May Bank holiday a month after Mum came home I got a phone call from Jean's care home saying that Jean had been confused and was resting and not to visit that day. The following day Trevor's sister drove from her home in Maidstone to see Jean. When she got there she saw that

Jean may have had a stroke but had not seen a doctor. Lynda insisted a doctor be called to examine Jean and voiced her concerns.

Lynda went back home that afternoon, but the next day, we got a call from the home saying that Jean had suffered a massive stroke that had rendered her blind and deaf. Jean had a phobia about hospitals all her life, so luckily she was not aware of her surroundings, but it made it difficult to communicate with her and calm her down. Due to her deafness, she would shout when talking and if someone approached her abruptly she screamed out.

I made Trevor visit his mum with me every evening after he'd had his meal. Mum was happy to be left at home alone and was really upset at Jean's predicament.

Jean was deteriorating, she would not drink or eat and needed bed baths which she hated and screamed at the interference. Lynda would only visit if her husband came with her. Luke would visit when he thought it was necessary and it was left up to us to do our bit, which considering my situation at home with Mum was quite a lot for me to do and selfish of Trevor's siblings.

When we visited I would sit and hold Jean's hand, stroking it at times and always saying 'I love you, Mum' when we left. The day before she passed she actually told me she loved me. Whether she knew it was me I don't know.

It was the middle of July and a weekend when I suddenly felt that we should ring the hospital before our visit. Jean had seemed so close to passing the night before I just knew something was going to happen. Luke had not visited her for some time, and I persuaded Trevor to ring his brother and advise him that it would be better if he visited Jean before the evening visits. He didn't want to change his plans and said that Jean had been going to pass away for the last week.

I was so upset with him, he would regret his decision and there was nothing we could do. At 4:00 pm that afternoon the hospital rang us to say that Jean had passed away peacefully. When Trevor rang Luke to tell him the news there was a long silence and then a thank you for ringing.

From the time Jean was moved from the family home and into the sheltered housing flat I was encouraged by Trevor, Luke and Lynda to look after the finances, hospital and GP appointments. That was ok until my parents moved down close to us then I was juggling with everything. Nothing was ignored at home and Trevor's responsibilities were still his job with some visits to his mum.

Trevor and I had booked the hotel for the wake and invited all the relatives, just under thirty in all, and we also brought my mum who in the end the two Mum's had grown quite fond of each other. I had typed and printed the order of service and had a picture on the front cover, and we also instructed Jean's solicitor in East Grinstead to sort out the financial side of things as she had been the one to organise Jean's will.

Trevor and I were not aware that when Terry passed away Luke got Jean to sign paperwork to the effect that they now co-owned the house. When the house was put up as part of Jean's estate Luke contested the decision and tried to stop it from taking place. His solicitor was contacted by Jean's solicitor and things came out that horrified us.

To cut a long story short once more, it was decided that the estate would be portioned between the three of Jean's children, which was a lifeline for us because Trevor had been made redundant again and was out of work. It had always been Terry's wish that the property when both parents passed away would be divided in equal share between the three siblings. Unfortunately, with the paperwork being presented by Luke's solicitor proved that something had been changed without Lynda or Trevor being made aware.

Jean had signed paperwork after Terry's death which meant that the property was owned by both Luke and Jean and this was against Terry's wishes. Once all the legal rang lings were sorted and to save Luke and Rose more solicitor problems the property was sold and each sibling receiving a fair share of the proceeds. It was a very unhappy, nasty and hurtful period for Trevor and me.

Rose had written me a letter which was very hurtful and insulting and trying to make me feel guilty. All this animosity from their part had been of their making and theirs alone. You reap what you sow.

According to Jean's solicitor, Rose and Luke moved far away to start a new life with their two children. To this day I do not know where that is I just hope they have been able to find peace and happiness in their new surroundings.

Trevor's Sister Lynda was not totally blameless and nearly got herself in real hot water. According to the solicitor acting for Jean's estate, a woman had contacted the bank and solicitor that Luke and Rose were dealing with in order to find out about Luke's estate. When this was divulged to us we were horrified, and we were asked to tell the person if we knew them that they had narrowly escaped prosecution, how they knew it was Lynda I do not know, but we did relay the information.

Whilst Jean's estate was being finalised my mum became more incapacitated and I'd asked the surgery for a nurse to help me care for Mum once a day. The trouble was having such a large property, everyone thought we had lots of money, but we were robbing Peter to pay Paul and constantly getting reminders from creditors about late payments. Then the threatening phone calls started coming fast and furious. I would not let Mum know the situation as she would have blamed herself.

She contributed as much as she could, but her Pension Credit had been halved because she was living with us. The high earning job in London that Trevor originally had was gone and the wages he was being offered down south was a lot less. Then at Christmas 2007, Trevor became ill and the GP called it exhaustion and signed him off work for two weeks. Oh God, the home became a mini-hospital juggling the medication, running errands and trying to do all the usual jobs around the huge bungalow and grounds.

Anyway, I struggled with Mum, and we were going out less and less. Mum's mood had changed, and I was working hard to keep her spirits up. I was beginning to get nervous in the mornings as to whether she may have passed away in the night. Then one morning I was taking a shower before she was up, and I heard Mum call me repeatedly and franticly.

I'd never got dried and dressed so quickly in all my life. I went into her room, and she was not able to move her legs and could not get out of bed. I half-carried her to the bathroom so she could have her morning visit.

Her health was fast going downhill, and at Christmas, I had hired from the mobility shop a wheelchair to ferry Mum back and forth from room to room. She hated it but knew she had no choice. I rang the surgery for some advice from the

GP, and she said Mum had no choice but to go into the cottage hospital at Horsham which was just up the road from us.

Mum refused to go, and I had to promise that it was only until they got her medications balanced as they had done before. I promised that I would bring her home once that was done. I truly believed that and that was why I had made her that promise. To make it less traumatic I drove her to the hospital.

After they settled, Mum into a single room the doctor came to see us and explained they would be doing blood tests and tweaking Mum's medication. I kissed Mum saying 'I love you' and left her quite happy, and I promised to visit that evening. As I was going out of her room the doctor asked to speak to me. He told me that there was nothing they could do for Mum and she'd be receiving palliative care.

I asked what it was and as he explained the full horror of my failed promise to Mum hit me, his words were distant, and I felt I had let her down I just wanted to go back in and take her home. With tears in my eyes, I drove home crying uncontrollably. Trevor thought Mum had passed away when he saw what I was like. I sobbed I just could not believe how quickly things had changed and were taken out of my hands.

It was February 2008, and Mum had been under my care for nearly five years, something none of us could have envisaged as she was originally given a maximum of six months to live. I thanked God for giving us some wonderful years and the chance for me to know who my mum really was. She was a gentle soul but with so much abuse all her life, and with my dad too I had found out, her opinion of people was distorted and being so family orientated she could not understand why Steven and his family were so detached from us and particularly why Alice had chosen to move so far away.

Once I realised how quickly Mum's health was changing I contacted Alice and Steven. Alice did get to see Mum then travelled back home. Steven came to visit her the evening before his birthday. He surprised her and us, but she was so glad to have seen the grandchildren.

Not that she had told me, she refused to speak to me or even look at me when I did go in every day. She would turn her back on me and never speak. Then as she became less mobile in bed she would hide her eyes. I never stopped talking to her, but I had inadvertently noticed while the nurse was arranging the bedclothes that Mum's legs had gone black from lack of circulation.

This told me she was now close to leaving us. Mum had accused me of getting her admitted because Trevor and I wanted time on our own. I nearly laughed in her face but realised it would be the wrong thing to do. Placating her was wrong, agreeing with her was wrong. Anything I said or did was wrong, and she would never forgive me.

Her last few days were so hurtful to me, and I summoned my brother Albert and told him to come and visit as I was not sure how long Mum had. The morning after Steven had visited Mum I visited Mum to see if she needed anything and tell her that Albert was coming to visit that morning. When I arrived Mum was on her back mumbling and talking to people but ignored me. I knew she was not long for this world and her soul would be free.

As my sister-in-law came into the room I said I needed to get some bits from home, and I would be back. I had already been with Mum for three hours that morning. Albert was parking the car and Joan his wife was talking to Mum telling her that Albert was just coming in. As he entered the room Mum opened her eyes and smiled at them and was gone.

At that time, I was coming out of the bungalow and locking the door when all of a sudden this forceful energy blew through me and nudged me, I instantly knew Mum had gone. As I arrived at the hospital car park and entered reception Joan came to warn me about Mum and I interrupted and said, "She's gone, I know."

Joan was stunned and wondered how I had known, and I then told her what had happened to me as I was closing the front door. It was my mum's way of saying goodbye, and hopefully, thank you.

Mum had passed away on Steven's birthday eight years to the day that they had been burgled in their London home, and she was buried six days later. I had a huge problem at hand because a few years previous Mum had made me promise that I would not let my brother Louis attend her funeral. Knowing what a nasty piece of work he was and the warning he had given me at Dad's funeral I was struggling to do the right thing by everyone.

In the end, I had decided to let Louis know about Mum by writing him a letter, and I posted it the day before Mum's funeral. I was hoping that it would not make him angry with me even more, because by the time the letter reached him in the Alps Mum would have got her wish and Louis would still be told about her death and the funeral arrangements. I had also mentioned in the letter that due to his not wanting to speak to me I had no choice but to write and let him know the news.

This may sound really insensitive to some of you, but I decided that everyone should come back to the bungalow after the funeral. I had prepared food and asked everyone to choose some items of Mum's. It would not be possible to get everyone together again in the very near future especially with Alice now living so far away.

Mum had accumulated over the past five years a huge amount of soft toys and a lot of these were taken for Joan's grandchildren. Steven took items for the girls Melisa and Hillary. Everyone went home with items to remember Mum and hopefully Dad too.

A couple of weeks after the funeral, I spent a lot of time clearing up the remainder of Mum's soft toys to give to the local children's charity. Some bits of furniture were sold other bits we kept. We approached estate agents to value the bungalow and as it was in good decorative order and carpeted throughout, we would get a good price for it. Trevor had found another job and was still only concentrating on his work, and I was managing everything else.

I'd decided to start selling our possessions and some furniture too. I would also have to sell all of my craft materials from the part-time mail-order business I had set up at home to earn some extra money. As we were on the main route out of town I put boards up advertising the garage sale.

As time went on the money from the garage sale was helping to reduce our debts. His health was not too brilliant, and he was not able to help me with maintaining the grounds.

I decided in order to give Trevor a break we would go away for a few days towards Devon/Cornwall and see what area we would be drawn to for our next move after the sale of the bungalow. This proved a nightmare as Trevor was getting more unwell and as we were making plans to make our way back home, I got a phone call on my mobile from Joan saying that Albert was in hospital in St Thomas's having had a heart attack.

At that point, I felt like I had been on a rollercoaster for the best part of my life just waiting for it to stop so that I could get off and be given the chance to live free of hassles.

In August, after Mum passed away, Trevor was made redundant again, and because he was now sixty, the dole office suggested he go on Pension Credit and that we should talk to the Citizens Advice Office. Trevor and I were shocked, was this going to be the end of his working life? How would we manage, where would we get the money from? The inheritance from Trevor's mum paid some of our outstanding debts and literally kept the wolves from the door. I went full steam ahead with having many more garage sales and with the For Sale sign outside more people came for a bargain and it suited me.

Trevor would at times come out and talk to some of the viewers otherwise he would be inside watching television. Basically, he had given up and everything was in my lap 'no surprise there then'.

One evening we were sitting watching television, and I just could not settle, I was literally like a jack in the box. I would get up then sit down. So nervous, but I did not know what about. The following day I had not settled but had calmed down a bit more.

The next day the neighbour saw us and told us his brother who lived upstairs had passed away, and they had not known until twenty-four hours later. As soon as we were told I knew that was why I had been so nervous. Since that time I have experienced this several times more and all with the same results. It is something I really do not like experiencing.

In October, Trevor was complaining of a strong pain at the back of his knee and as it went on for a whole day I took him to the GP, and she diagnosed DVT (deep vein thrombosis), I knew that was bad. We had to go to Crawley Hospital to have a scan to determine the problem.

On his arrival, Trevor had a DVT scan that showed a blood clot, and he was given an injection in the stomach and more to do by himself at home. He also had to wear pressure knee-length socks. Anyone who has experienced these muscle demanding garments will know what a pain in the proverbial they are.

By the Christmas of that year, Trevor was off all the medication and was given the all-clear. Still, his health was not good, and he could not cope with any day to day events at home. Everything seemed to put him on edge or scare him.

If the phone rang he would jump and say you get that. I honestly thought he was having a nervous breakdown.

In January 2009, we went back to see the GP, and she made an appointment for Trevor to see a consultant at Redhill. I thought this is good we are doing the runs of hospitals I had frequented Redhill hospital when my mum needed treatment.

Before I tell you what happened, I need to say that I have the greatest of respect for all medical officials. Consultants, doctors, nurses and far more, they train for many years and should be listened to when you are given the opportunity to get an appointment with them as they are trying their best to improve your health.

We arrived at the reception and handed the appointment letter over. The reception was full, but we managed to find two vacant seats. We waited a considerable time I even went to reception hoping we had not been missed. I was reassured that the appointments diary was full for that day, but we were next in.

Trevor was calm as a cucumber, he always had been, he could be screaming inside or being really scared, but he never showed it. He kept everything inside, always bottling things up and never sharing any thoughts or emotions. Anyway, half an hour later, we were called to see the Consultant.

Bloods had been taken the week before the surgery, and Trevor and I had been to the local hospital for Trevor to have a CT scan. We entered the consulting room and shook hands with the consultant and were asked to sit down.

The consultant talked about the CT scan which was on his screen giving us all the usual jargon they spout out at you as though they are talking to a colleague rather than a patient. I stopped him in his tracks and said can you tell us what it is Trevor has come to see you about. Until that visit for weeks and weeks, nobody would tell us what the problem was. He stopped, looked puzzled and said, "Were you not told by your GP what the appointment was for?" We both shook our heads.

Then in a matter of fact way, he said, "Well, you have Parkinson's."

Due to the manner in which he gave us the news we still were not aware of how serious the illness was. Trevor and I looked at each other and asked, "What is Parkinson's?"

The consultant started to explain, and I said that we should have a second opinion, and he promptly told Trevor to go outside the room and walk up and down the corridor (I thought this bloke is having a laugh, what's going on?). As soon as Trevor had walked half the length of the corridor he asked Trevor to come back into the room, and he was sure that it was Parkinson's.

I was not happy with his laid back attitude and posture, he was nearly laying down with his feet up on the desk whilst talking to us, and I still asked for a second opinion. He replied, "The test is very expensive."

I asked, "Do we have to pay for it?"

"No, the surgery would."

"That's ok; then we'll have it," I said.

Having waited another few weeks for the test then the result, in March 2009, it was confirmed that Trevor had got Parkinson's. The sale of the bungalow was not going well and with the news that Trevor had got Parkinson's, we were still trying to come to terms with this so we decided to drop the asking price considerably and within months we were once again travelling around the south looking for an area that would draw us in. We found it, Bournemouth.

For a change, I was now making all the decisions and Trevor had no choice. Steven and his family did not visit us very often, and he was doing what he always wanted. Alice had moved away as she was doing what she wanted. We were now going to do what was best for us.

It was years since we'd had a holiday and with all the pressures of life for so long I wanted us to have some sort of breather. We did not know how long Trevor would be mobile for, and we needed to enjoy life in some form or another.

Steven and the family came to visit one more time just before we moved and Nicola had the cheek to tell me that with us moving so far away the girls would miss us a lot. I nearly laughed in her face, but instead, I pointed out that she and Steven were leading the life they wanted, Alice was doing the same thing, and after all that, we had gone through all the past years we too were entitled to do what we wanted and what would be best for us for a change. There were no comments from either of them (I thought don't you dare put a guilt trip on me, darling; the children won't miss us as they never got use to us anyway).

Not long after Steven and Nicola had got married Nicola turned to me and said, "Your son is your son until he gets a wife, your daughter is your daughter for the rest of your life." That told me to back off and that he was no longer my son. Over my dead body, I thought—I don't think so darling.

My children would be mine until I'd died and beyond. It was so eerie because I had been told the same thing by Jean many years previous and my reply to her was that Trevor would always be her son no matter what and that she should not think any differently.

Although Bournemouth was a very busy place compared to where we had been living, we were going through the final stages with solicitors and booking removal men. In September 2009, we moved. I could not wait to put my feet up as Trevor had no strength to help with any of the packings. He would sit there feeling guilty that I was burdened with all the preparations and the packing.

I was dreading the driving not knowing what the traffic would be like and if the removal men were going to be there when we arrived. I did not feel excited just full of fear and trepidation and so uncertain of our future. This time though we would be free of debts for the first time in all of our thirty-six years of married life. We were heading to our new life in Bournemouth as pensioners in waiting with no income until then.

I still could not get used to the fact that I still did not have to speak to my parents regularly. There were no friends to leave behind, not even the neighbours. The five years in the bungalow had brought us the death of both the boys, Trevor's mum and my mum but also the ill health that Trevor was now facing, and of course, the constant discomfort I was experiencing on a daily basis with my lower back as a result of the two-car accidents.

Change for Trevor proved to be quite a challenge, but he seemed more relaxed. We had no mortgage worries as the sale of the bungalow managed to clear all our huge debts and left us a small sum that we would need for rent until we were in receipt of our State Pensions.

Bournemouth

The place we had moved to in Bournemouth was a semidetached house near the A338 leading into Bournemouth and it was quite noisy. Very soon we noticed that Trevor was having trouble with the stairs and with the rent being over £1000 per month we knew that within six months we had to find somewhere more suitable.

After familiarising ourselves with the areas around us, we started looking and taking more things into consideration when deciding where to live. Within weeks, we found it easy to drive around without getting lost.

Bournemouth had been a favourite of my brothers. Louis would always visit the area when he brought his family regularly to the surrounding campsites. Albert visited the area in his bachelor days and had nothing but praise for the area.

We were not drawn by any of the districts until we saw Christchurch and Trevor was taken by it a lot. We registered with an estate agent and all over again we were looking for our next home. While we were living in Bournemouth we were visited by the Parkinson's coordinator who gave us so many leaflets, phone numbers and also the details of the local Parkinson's group who met once a month in Christchurch.

If you remember, Trevor had always worked long hours, and we never managed as a couple to befriend neighbours on a social basis. I never had the chance to socialise with work colleagues either as I was always temping or working part-time. Basically, we never had a social life of any description.

So coming to another new environment, new neighbours and perhaps club members too was a whole new world to us and filled me with excitement as I had never had proper friends to socialise with, yes, I know Trevor was sixty-one, and I was fifty-nine. Trevor on the other hand was quite happy to live quietly and not have a social life. Dream on sunshine I thought.

Having decided on the new area we would like to live in we visited the town. There was a lot going for it with a small cottage hospital but no A & E that would have to be Bournemouth. A choice of supermarkets and other small shops appeared to have all you would need on a daily basis. It also offered numerous pubs and a theatre that we could look forward to visiting at some point.

After quite a lot of searching, we found a semidetached bungalow just outside the town, within walking distance of the hospital and close to a small parade of shops and a pub. When making our decision for our next home we also had to think of the future and what if I was not able to drive, how close to public transport would we be and so on.

You know when you get older and the children have moved out you try and 'downsize', well we had sold over two-thirds of our bungalow contents in Horsham. When we moved to Bournemouth, we found we still had too many possessions, and we downsized again with our living space and possessions. We passed on to Steven and Alice a lot of things they wanted to hold on to and what they didn't want we donated to charity.

Some furniture we kept in order to store possessions that could not go into the garage. Using the loft was not an option because I could not stand heights nor would I have been able to comfortably negotiate a ladder and the hatch.

In January 2010, within a couple of months of us being in the bungalow, my brother Albert rang me it was just before Christmas, and he was in quite a distress state and was saying that he was so desperate about things at home with his wife and her children. This was his second marriage with Joan, and she had four children. They could never spend time together as the children (all grown up with families of their own) were always having dramas and his wife would always pick them over what he wanted to do with the two of them.

On his days off, he would nearly always be driving one or the other to different places. There was always a drama to be solved, and he wasn't feeling right. He'd had this cough for about three months and would not go to the doctor. I just listened and gave advice about the doctor, but I just let him offload, and he had never done that before. I was really concerned.

Within and few weeks Joan rang to say the x rays showed Albert had got lung cancer, and he would be going for surgery as soon as they could find him a bed. He could not talk to me about it because he was so upset with me and the sadness I would feel at hearing his news. How right he was, Albert was admitted to the William Harvey in Kent for observation whilst awaiting surgery. Within days, I took a three-hour train journey from home to see my darling brother whom I had helped my mum to bring up.

In my heart, I knew this would be the last time I would see him, and I ached inside to cry my eyes out, but I prayed to God to help me keep it together, and I did. A few days later, I woke up in the middle of the night, and I was crying and immediately I knew Albert had gone. Shortly after I got a text from Joan to confirm what I already knew (I'm sorry, but this really upsets me to tell you. I need my hankie).

After speaking with Joan, it was agreed that I should try and contact my brother Louis in France. I no longer cared whether he was still angry with me or not, it was now nearly seven years since his threat to me so I rang to give him the news and when he answered, and I started to inform him, he said, "I already know," and put the phone down.

Well, that was easy I thought and then I smiled to myself and thought Albert had made it easy for me, bless him.

For Albert's funeral, Trevor and I went by car, and I drove. We stayed in a hotel overnight and went to Albert's house to be collected by the funeral car. Our son Steven was asked to be one of the pall-bearers, but he travelled in his own car from Crawley to Ashford. Alice was unable to attend as she could not get the time off work.

Albert had worked in the Mayor's office for eighteen years and was highly regarded by many. The Mayor's office asked that his funeral car should pass the front of the Civic offices where they had arranged for a lone bagpipe player to play. As we passed the Civic Offices many members of staff stood outside with heads bowed, and I think that was the best respect they could have shown Albert, and he would have been so proud.

Albert and Joan visited Scotland a few times to see friends who had moved up there. On their last trip, they were looking out over the vast countryside and Albert turned to Joan and said, "If I was to die today, I would be a happy man." That was the summer before he passed away.

Christchurch Home 1

After six months in Bournemouth, we moved into the bungalow, it had a large garden with a lot of grass that needed mowing, fruit trees and flower borders and a garage at the side where this time we stored all the excess possessions and managed to donate the furniture that we could not fit in our new home. There was a nice sized drive to the front with a low wall and a gate.

Very soon we got into a routine and Trevor was visiting the Parkinson's nurse at the hospital and finally accepting that he would need to start taking medication to help him manage to do things on a day to day basis.

Once Trevor was diagnosed in the summer of 2009, I quickly realised I was now responsible for Trevor and although our relationship had just been plutonic I would have moved heaven and earth to help him cope with his condition. His health and well-being was in my charge, and I had to do the very best for him and more if possible as I had done for all my other family members.

It was really funny because in the first months when we moved to Bournemouth, we were like two kids in a candy shop well I was more than Trevor. We had never been free of debt all our married lives and for just a brief moment (about eight months) we went to the theatre, ate meals at Harry Ramsdens, I would drive us to different places around, and at that time, Trevor still had his sense of direction and would navigate. We travelled to see Steven a few times as the Granddaughters would be dancing in different shows. We also travelled to Cheshire to visit Alice and her husband Darren. This to me was the high life.

Bournemouth at the time also had a tethered hot air balloon that could be seen on the skyline from a long distance. I was and still am terrified of heights, but Trevor and I went on it. The balloon rose to the height of four hundred ninety-two feet, and there was a running commentary about the one hundred and twenty miles distant views. We had only gone up a few feet and the balloon started swaying in the breeze, and I was looking down into the basket, and I started to cry.

Then I thought if I fixed my sight on a distant point that may help and it did, but I could not move I was frozen to the spot and still crying. The whole experience took about ten minutes. I was so proud that I had challenged myself Trevor had no height problems and enjoyed it immensely.

When Alice and Darren came down to visit she wanted to go up in the balloon, and Trevor and I went up again. No, it was still as scary as the first time, and I was still crying like a baby.

The following year when Alice had begun to realise Trevor's condition was changing she decided to abseil down the Liverpool Cathedral to raise money for Parkinson's research. Alice was just as scared of heights as I was and would not even climb a loft ladder at home. I could not bear to think of her doing the abseiling. Darren was allowed to go up with her and encourage her from the side gallery.

She managed to get out over the edge and froze. She said that at that moment she thought of her dad who would have that happen to him many times a day because of his Parkinson's and that spurred her on to make the descent. We were so proud of her, and she became our hero. Alice raised over £1000 for her courage.

It was on our last journey to Alice that I had realised Trevor's mind was not what it was, and he was sending me in different directions to where we needed to be. It took us ages to get to Alice and Darren's house.

It convinced me to have a sat nav, which was all the rage at the time. On the way home, Trevor still managed to argue the toss and tell me on many occasions that we were being sent the wrong way which wasn't the case.

After that, we made the next visit to Alice and Darren by train to Crew where Alice and Darren had picked us up in their car. This trip was definitely to be our last as it had taken its toll on Trevor's stamina. Also, as he had trouble with the stairs we had to book into the local hotel.

Life was becoming more and more difficult, coping with day to day things were kept to a minimum, and I had to stop involving Trevor in any of the housekeeping, finances and general running of our home. Everything I kept simple and to a minimum, I would always ask if he wanted to know about anything I was doing, and he would reply, "You know what you are doing, you know best."

Once when Trevor and I visited Salisbury, I heard bagpipes being played and it was a soldier playing well-known songs, and I just welled up and had to come away, I instinctively sensed that Albert was with us that day. Then quite recently, I was with a group from Age Concern in

Weymouth, and I was walking through the pedestrianised area looking at the shop windows, and in the distance, I heard the bagpipes.

I had to go and listen to that lovely music and again he was a soldier just playing to the public. I just had to put a donation in his cap in memory of my dear Albert and a smile came to my face as I did so. I still welled up and had to explain to those in my party why I was so upset. Albert was with me again on that day.

From autumn 2003 to spring 2010, I had lost my dad, the boys, my mother-in-law, my mum and now my brother Albert. Everyone I had come to England with, was now gone. I knew I would never see Louis again so for me he was gone too.

Trevor was finding life quite a strain, and I tried to reduce the amount of stuff we still had stored in the large garage. I had got to know our neighbour quite well. She was my height (small) and reminded me so much of my mum. She had a dog, and he was not too partial to visitors.

We would have such laughs, real belly laughs you know? I had decided that with the large drive at the front of the bungalow I could have a garage sale so I asked Ruth if she wanted to share my drive. We had a garage sale a couple of times, and I managed to get rid of all the stuff bar a few bits that went to the charity shops.

Ruth being a hoarder managed to sell quite a bit but would also sell at boot fairs and got rid of her family bits there. Trevor was not impressed and kept a low profile and made us a cup of tea when asked, but I would have to collect it from the kitchen as he was not able to carry them out to us.

Something that I had only experienced a few times whilst on family holidays with my mum was playing bingo. We would win so many things. For once I just wanted to try Gala bingo, and I asked Ruth if she would like to go with us.

The first time we went none of us managed to get to grips with it. I know I can hear you saying, it's only numbers you cover-up. Yes, but they go really fast so that you miss numbers, and I was helping Trevor who just got so tied up that he gave up and Ruth and I had to try and cover his numbers too.

After that, Trevor did not want to go but was not too pleased with Ruth and me going together. Who does that remind you of? We did this a few times and then I found Trevor had not taken medication at the right time and it all got too much for me to cope with and spoilt it all for me, so we didn't go anymore.

Since moving to the bungalow, I had decided that renting privately was going to take the bulk if not all our savings and after speaking to the Parkinson's nurse we went to the local council and put our names on the waiting list for housing. We would have to be on it for a minimum of three years before being considered. That was fair, but at least we had a foot in the door and something to fall back on when eventually many years from then we may need help with housing.

In April 2011, we used some of the remainders of our savings and be booked the whole family on a trip to Guernsey for a week including flights, breakfast and an evening meal. I knew that very soon Trevor would no longer be able to travel and this would be our last holiday with the children and grandchildren. Not that we'd had one before, but you know what I mean.

Trevor and I drove to Steven's house and parked our car there. We all got transport to Gatwick airport and on the flight to Guernsey. Alice and Darren travelled from Manchester to Guernsey, and we all met up at the Guernsey Airport.

The flight for me was a white knuckle ride as the plane was an 'elastic band one' (propellers). My reaction and crying too was amusing my granddaughters who were used to travelling by plane.

The hotel I had chosen was like a Swiss Chalet high up with its own beach. Not having a car proved quite a strain for Trevor so he, and I would travel by bus to the main town and have a stroll around and the rest of the family pleased themselves. We met for breakfast and evening meal.

A couple of days before we were going home Darren had words with the manager who owned an old Harley Davidson motorbike. Trevor knew my passion for these bikes and the fact that I was prepared to pay an owner for a five-minute tour just to say I had ridden one. As I came out of the lift with Trevor Alice and Darren were waiting for us in reception and the Manager was standing behind the desk and turned to me and said, "Would you mind helping me to take some items to the post office please."

I thought what an odd thing to ask a guest.

I was encouraged to go by Alice and Darren, Trevor did not know what was going on, and I thought any minute now he is going to say no you are not going. As I went outside the Manager gave me a helmet, and I looked at him puzzled and said, "What's this for; where is your car?"

He replied, "I thought you might like to ride on the Harley instead."

I was crying; Alice and Darren were too because they knew how excited I was.

The manager helped me with the helmet and said come on we are wasting bike time. We took off, and I just could not believe my excitement and fear of falling off. The sound of the bike was just unbelievable. We eventually got to the main sorting office, and he told me to stay on the bike whilst he went in.

I dare not move because with my weight on the back the bike tilted so much that I thought I would fall off. I will never forget the Manager's kindness and Alice and Darren's thoughtfulness in helping me to full fill one of my dreams. I forgot to tell you, that summer would be my sixtieth birthday. The whole family had a great time, and afterwards, we received in the post a spiral-bound memory book of photos of our holiday on the Island, another lovely surprise.

At the end of 2011, I had convinced Trevor that we should try and join the local Parkinson's help group it wasn't far from home and by now we had a Motability car so a lot of the worry from my point of view was gone. I had to give my lovely little car to the garage as a deposit for the Motability car we had chosen (sorry Trevor had chosen). It had so many gadgets, vision all round was more restricted, and basically, I hated it. For the first week, I cried because I just did not like to have to re-learn all the positions of the controls, and yes, I had air con in this one, and I knew where the control for that was.

Trevor just could not fathom out my thinking. Had he been in a position to drive the car he would have been in heaven. I just wanted my little car my very first proper car that I had chosen new from the dealers. Micra was the one that took me to so many places and helped me to help others on hundreds of occasions. From then on the car I drove was just an object of transport for Trevor, and I was the chauffeur.

The Parkinson's group was lovely, and the couple that ran it were really nice and helpful. As the weeks went on, Trevor was talking more softly than usual, and he was making me feel that I was going deaf. The GP decided to book him in with the speech therapist at the local hospital for six weeks for one-hour sessions. It was great because I could have some me-time.

When he had finished the sessions he was more audible and even the group members noticed the difference. He would always ask me what had I been doing while he was in the unit. Keeping tabs on me, it never stopped.

Trevor was being asked by some of the members at the Parkinson's group as to what the sessions had been like, so I decided to type up a one-page leaflet about his experience and the therapy, and I printed some copies to hand around to those interested. Then Trevor had his name put down for the day hospital locally again where he learnt how to use a rollator safely, how to walk and try and manage his low blood pressure, a condition that many suffer from with Parkinson's.

Trevor was also having trouble turning over in bed, and I found fitted satin sheets did the job. All of these things I put into a 'Did you know' newsletter for the group, and they loved it and expected something every month. I was happy to do it and some of the bits I would get from the newspapers and magazines, and with the group leaders' permission, we gave it a go. I involved Trevor and made him feel important and it also gave me something different to think about.

Towards the end of 2011, Trevor was struggling to get in and out of the bath, and I asked the landlord if there was any chance of changing the bath for a shower. It was not possible, and we had to look to move again. So we moved and downsized again. All I could think of was that more money was being spent on removals and agency fees in such a short space of time. We eventually found a small one-bed ground floor flat by the Park and closer to the town centre.

Christchurch Home 2

In spring 2012, two and a half years after moving to Dorset we moved into the flat. It was the smallest home we had lived in, and we both found it very claustrophobic. It was damp so a dehumidifier was bought and used constantly and it was also noisy from all the traffic on the main road. There was a bathroom and a very small shower room.

To begin with, things were ok, and with my help, Trevor could shower ok, but within six to seven months he was struggling to stand long enough for me to wash him. I bought a number of different stalls for him to sit on, but they made him stick out of the shower cubicle so much that the floor got really wet each time. We had also been on the council waiting list for nearly three years by now, and we had run out of money.

Social services came to assess Trevor and tried to get a stall installed, but that too was no good. The landlord would not fix a small stall against the back wall so we had to move again. Social services put us on a list to be re-housed to suitable accommodation within the community. The panel that made these decisions met each month and considered which applicant was most in need. At the first panel meeting, our application was rejected.

I was getting really desperate, so I asked social services to book us someone to come and visit and see what Trevor was going through each day. Then I got the GP, Parkinson's consultant, the nurse and the day hospital to write saying how Trevor's health was changing so quickly and for them to write in support of my request for council housing help.

They all did their bit and all the correspondence I received I gave to social services for the next panel meeting, but we had to wait another month on from that because we had missed that month's meeting by a few days.

A week after the next panel meeting we got a phone call from a housing association asking if we would like to visit a complex in the Christchurch area with carers on sight, our details had been put forward to them by the Council. We agreed to the appointment and met with the young girl from lettings, and we went up in the lift. We got out on the second floor and it was all very quiet but bright. As she opened the door to the flat it took my breath away the pure bright sunshine shone through every room as the flat-faced south and it was so welcoming a huggable warm feeling throughout.

As we were being shown around, she came to the second bedroom, and I quickly said, "Oh no, I don't believe it, your offering us a two-bed flat and the council have got us down for a one-bed flat."

She replied, "Do you and your husband like the flat?"

We both beamed and said a big 'YES'.

"Sign on the dotted line and it is yours."

I just burst into tears, we could just about afford the rent and it was so spacious and no gardening either woohoo! What I had not been told until much later, the second bedroom was because of Trevor's Parkinson's, sometime in the future

Trevor would need hoists and a different bed and more equipment. But for now, my only concern was moving and being able to afford the cost.

Whilst living at the bungalow and attending the Parkinson's group we met a lady who was a member of the coffee morning group at the same hall where the Parkinson's group met and this too was on a Thursday but in the mornings. The coffee morning group was quite large with people of all ages from the mid-50s upwards.

From that, we also managed to hear about the Age Concern group who met every Wednesday afternoon at the same hall and played bingo, had outings, speakers and were always looking for new members. A minibus would bring some from further afield.

One lady Sharon who went to the coffee morning and owned a small van volunteered her services for the main bulk of our removal. We managed to move all the boxed items and small fragile bits and the removal firm would take the large furniture and heavy items. It took Sharon and me two trips in her van, and we were so grateful, and in early summer of 2013, we moved in.

Christchurch Home 3

Once settled in, I passed Sharon's details round to the residents, and she managed to sell her crafts at the home once every three weeks at the coffee morning. We also gave her a load of unwanted items which she managed to sell at boot fairs, and she also had the two-year-old washing machine we would no longer need.

Instead of getting carpets down, we used the cushion flooring that was already in place and gave it a good scrub. It turned out to be the best idea I'd had in a long time. The summers were getting hotter and the flat facing south meant the rooms were extremely warm most of the time. The heating was on only a couple of months of the year.

The building was managed by a big housing association, and they also provided the care staff and carried out all the maintenance too. We simply could not have asked for more. The only thing was, in the first couple of weeks, in the quiet, I would cry and cry because having just turned sixty-two and in reasonable health, I did not really want to end my days in a care home. This sacrifice I was once again making for Trevor.

Residents were in this complex for different health reasons, some had just stayed on as their husband or wife had passed away. Some were in wheelchairs, using rollators or walking aids. Others had dementia, learning difficulties or needed nursing care or reminding to take their medication. There was a laundry room with all the facilities including ironing board and iron, then a small room where the hairdresser visited once a week.

For those energetic enough, there was a room with exercise bikes and a treadmill. The massive lounge had a dining area to one side with views and a door to the well-kept gardens at the back. The dining room seated thirty-two and one side a large kitchen for staff to give out the meals and a small kitchen next to that for residents to use on a daily basis. Meals were brought in by an outside caterer.

The remaining large area with windows to the road lead to other buildings and the nursing home along the road, the lounge area was peppered with comfortable armchairs and small coffee tables. By the television, some armchairs accommodated residents wanting to watch television in the evenings and sometimes at lunchtime. There was also a couple of heavily stocked bookshelves and a music centre for CDs and radio listening.

Trevor thought that once we were settled in our new home we'd keep ourselves to ourselves and go out as and when we pleased. I had different ideas. This was the first time in my life I'd had the chance of making proper friends other than my previous next-door neighbour from the bungalow.

I asked the manager if we could have a House Warming party and invite all the residents and get the chance to meet them, and they would meet us. Karen thought it was a great idea and hoped it would create a good response from the residents.

I did all the food and even baked a large cake. We set the tables out and had soft drinks or tea and coffee. To get Trevor to join in my mad idea I invited Ruth along with Mary and Alan husband and wife who we got to know at the Parkinson's group. Trevor sat with them like Mr Grumpy and not wanting to meet anyone, and I laughed and joked with residents and got the staff to join in with us too.

Karen the manager was so pleased to see some of the residents who did not like to mix or take part in anything suddenly appear as they had actually managed to come down and joined in. Everyone said what a brilliant idea it was and thanked us for our thoughtfulness.

After we had cleared up and gone back to the flat, I was buzzing and so happy I could have jumped out of the window and flew. Trevor could not understand my exuberance. I had never been to a party, never organised one or met so many prospective friends. Wow, how great was this life going to be? I could face anything now nothing was going to burst my bubble.

Then it suddenly dawned on me, Trevor would not be happy that I would have friends, he wanted me home and with him. Oh dear, my dad came to mind when he got angry at Mum having my company when they moved closer to me. History was repeating itself all over again.

Oh, what's the phrase I'm looking for? Yes, I know 'there is always one fly in the ointment' and I shall call him Spoiler because he was a person who managed to make resident's lives miserable and would strut along the corridors as though he owned the building and everyone in it. He was a thorn on many people's sides.

Spoiler had been part of a residents association that had been disbanded for some reason or another. Later on, he had managed to resurrect the association under a different name and rules and got residents involved in running it with him at the helm.

Some residents were new to the complex and did not really know what he was like. He was literally power-mad but had no empathy with residents and only did things to make himself look good and when it did not go his way he would suddenly have an attack of some sort so that residents would feel sorry for him.

I have no wish to describe his character or spend any more time on him, I will say one thing he was the most evil and manipulative person I had ever had the misfortune to meet and was one of my biggest challenges in life to date.

As the weeks went by and I got to know more residents, it became quite apparent that many of my new friends did not see relatives very often and some never went out only by taxi to the hospital or surgery. That broke my heart, and I was desperate to find something for them to look forward to from time to time.

Now I know many of you will relate to what I am going to tell you, whether you have joined an association, a club, a charity or go into a place like ours. There will always be someone who will come up to you giving you the impression that they are helping you and proceed to tell you all about who and why you should avoid or be aware of. When nine times out of ten they are one of those you will eventually have trouble with.

They were a mother and daughter who were very close to Spoiler and were happy to support him with any of his 'get popular schemes'. By the way, does this part of my recollecting not remind you of our school days?

All my life I had been a keen photographer. With this in mind, I asked the Manager Karen if I could produce a calendar to raise funds for the home and that money could go to hiring a beach hut by the sea. I had made enquiries with the booking office at the beach, also found out all the charges and fees, worked out the taxi fare to and from the home and my idea was that the cabin could be used by any resident.

I was given the green light and proceeded to ask the opinion of the residents, everyone was ready to buy a calendar there and then. Green light again, this was really promising. I went to the local printers and got quotes for five hundred calendars the minimum they would print and it would cost £1,100. (We had not got a windfall it was a pension Trevor had cashed in to keep us going and some of that money I borrowed to pay for the calendars.) The calendars had to be produced to get them sold, taking orders was not an option, and I would have also needed to sell them outside of the home too to get them all sold.

The photos I would be using were taken from visits Trevor, and I had made on our walkabouts in Christchurch and on the back of the calendar was printed the reason for producing the calendar. It was A4 in full colour with little descriptive titles of the place pictured. Green lights all the way. All the printer needed to do was to replicate what I had produced; this was the best way as it cut the costs down dramatically.

To encourage the sale of the calendar with the residents and their family and friends I made a four-foot poster in the shape of a beach hut with horizontal lines each marking £50 already in the pot. Everyone was so excited.

Unbeknown to me Spoiler had gone into the office and informed Karen that I was not allowed to sell or handle any money given by the residents he went as far as to inform the Landlords of my plans.

The trouble was I had already placed the order and paid. I was getting it in the neck from Trevor thinking we would lose our money and Spoiler was trying to trip me up at every turn.

So it was agreed that the office would hold the money, and I would keep the records of sales. No Spoiler said that the office was only allowed to hold petty cash and not 'substantial' amounts of cash.

So then Trevor and I decided to get a five-lever lock put on a large cupboard/room in our flat to the cost of £115.00, and this was agreed by residents and Karen so that was that. Spoiler was stopped in his tracks. The months that all this took place made Trevor very nervous and anxious.

At the coffee morning, there had been discussions about the meals being provided to the home and many residents did not like the quality of the food on offer and refused to come down to lunch. Trevor and I had tried the food on our first week but only tried two meals, and it was really bad.

I and some of the other residents shouted him down and said how could he advocate the meals as he never came down to eat them. He was furious and so angry that he wrote a letter to all residents stating that I had stirred up trouble about the meals and the provider. I was forced to reply but politely and truthfully about his misrepresentation of me and what had taken place. One thing I was wrong in doing was to mention the lack of meal choices, and I also called the meals 'slop', which everyone privately agreed with but would not put their name to. I gave all the residents a copy as he had done with his letter.

He hit the roof and to this day I still do not know what he told the acting manager on duty that day, but it was a Saturday morning at 9:00 am, and both Trevor and I jumped out of our skins as she banged and banged and banged on our flat door. Thinking it was a resident in distress I ran to open the door and it was Margaret the acting manager. She was shouting and screaming at me and telling me that I had no right to send the letter to the residents and how dare I do this.

There were vulnerable residents in the building, and they could be upset. I calmed her down reminding her that it was a Saturday morning and that she should come inside and tell me what the problem was. Trevor was shaking thinking we were going to be thrown out. Once Margaret had stated her objection to my letter she went, not before reminding her that Trevor was a vulnerable resident too and that she had overlooked that fact when she went into her attack on us.

Trevor was shaking for some time and really worried about the situation to the point that we had an argument about my letter. I reminded him that I had been bullied all my life, and I was drawing the line here and how I had told the truth, and I was not going to back down and no we were not going to be thrown out.

It took me all weekend to calm Trevor down to the point that we bought a doorbell and stuck a notice on the door for callers not to use the knocker but to please ring the bell.

Unbeknown to us Spoiler had on that weekend emailed the manager Karen, the Area Manager Louise and anybody else he could think of in an attempt to get us ousted whilst still on our probationary period (Not a chance I said to myself). On Monday morning, I went to see the manager and explained what had taken place.

Also that the acting manager that day had been out of order in talking to me in that manner, scaring my husband witless and taking sides when she had not had all the facts to hand. Karen and I knew this was a serious misconduct issue. I could have taken it further, but I had no wish to as I knew she had been stirred up by Spoiler.

The following day the Area Manager came to see me and asked if with Karen present they could have a meeting with us in our flat about this issue. Meanwhile, Spoiler was standing back waiting to get what he was hoping for, for us to be put on a warning. In your dreams sunshine, you'll have to try harder than that.

That afternoon Karen and Louise the area manager came in all very polite and sat listening to both Trevor and me pointing out how badly we were treated by the acting manager and falsely accused of something we had not done. They could see how scared Trevor was. I also explained that my letter was just a reply from me to the letter he had given to residents the day before. WHAT LETTER? They both jumped up and asked, I had Spoiler's letter and offered them a copy which they read.

The meeting was stopped as they took the letter away, this stopped them in their tracks, and they left. Now the staff could not lose face, the acting manager was moved to another site, and I was asked to apologise for saying things in the letter which Spoiler did not like, including the word describing the meals. They were true, but he did not like it. I told Karen and

Louise I would not apologise even if we lost our flat. I was not going to be bullied, and I had told the truth.

What none of us knew at that point was that Spoiler had chosen to send a copy of my letter to the caterer responsible for the horrible meals. The caterer took umbrage and wanted an apology as this was slander. After discussions going back and forth, Trevor and I had to meet with the caterer and to make sure we apologised Mary Spoiler's close friend offered to 'support' us in the meeting (Yeh right, she wanted to see us grovel to the caterer).

Well, we did no such thing. I apologised for his taking it the wrong way, I stood by what I had said and told him that in future, I would keep my opinions to myself. He seemed happy at that, and we left the meeting, but Spoiler never got an apology from us.

When the calendars came out they sold really quickly and Spoiler was always in the corners observing the sales and even got one of his 'friends' to purchase a copy. The money guide was going up and up and residents were getting excited. Spoiler informed the office that having the chart in the foyer was not conducive to the overall look of the home so I had to remove it, but I gave regular updates to the residents at coffee morning once a week. At that point, I was starting to wonder who was actually running the complex.

I managed to sell the calendars to a lot of our club members at Parkinson's, our outside coffee morning group, hairdressers, local church gift shop, and I even hired a table inside the local theatre/cinema on a couple of Saturdays and even the care home along the road bought some, I tried as much as I could to push the sales, even though I was Trevor's carer 24/7, and he was against it all and never gave me any moral support.

All the residents at the home had become more aware of the dark side that Spoiler was showing, and they did not like it, especially that Trevor and I had been willing to put up the funds to get the calendars printed. Anyway, all the calendars were eventually sold, but in the time, it took me to sell the calendars we lost our slot for hiring a beach hut so all the residents decided that we should all have a great Christmas Party with entertainers the lot. Yes, bring it on I thought.

I managed to organise a two-course dinner with the help of the activities coordinator all prepared in the small resident's kitchen and mine. I had decided to take the stage II Food Hygiene Certificate as this was something Spoiler was going to try and use to stop me from organising the food for the party. I made up all the menus, invitations, tickets and posters and printed them myself.

We had over thirty-five seated for the meal plus staff giving me a hand when they were free. We sold raffle tickets for the large raffle (prizes supplied by the residents) and for a couple of weeks before, there was a buzz in the complex and most residents were on a high and so looking forward to the evening.

I and a couple of the staff decided to give everyone a laugh and as part of the entertainment we dressed up with all in one costumes mine was a tiger and the two staff had bought themselves tutus to add to their leopard costumes, but I made mine to match the orange and black outfit. I wore a reindeer hairband over the hood and Pixie puffed up green slippers with bells on. The two staff members were not pleased as my outfit looked miles better than theirs, and we had a good laugh about it. It was time for us to be really stupid and make them all laugh.

Our time came one resident put our music on (Everybody Needs Somebody to Love) from the Blues Brothers. We came in singing and dancing and making idiots of ourselves and the residents were in stitches. We also had chocolates that we were throwing to the audience and the next thing I know I slipped because my large Pixie green slippers were smooth on the soles (I know they did not match but being only five feet tall my nickname was Pixie) and it added a touch of humour.

So I slipped and within a second I was on my back and not wishing to spoil things I immediately flapped my arms up and down whilst laying there, feeling no broken bones I got up quickly and carried on with the jigging about. No one person realised I had slipped and thought I had put it into the act. 'What, I'm not that brave'.

Everyone had a brilliant night and the money raised from the raffle would go towards another activity. On Christmas day of that year 2014, there would have been quite a few residents alone in their rooms as family were not taking them out. It broke my heart and much against Trevor's wishes I approached the residents in turn and invited those that would be alone to have Christmas dinner with us, and I would be cooking, but there ended up being twelve in those sad circumstances, and we could not have them all in our flat.

With Karen's permission, I then decided to set the tables out in the dining hall, and I decorated the tables and with funds bought boxes of chocolates from the pound shop and wrapped them up and placed them at each setting so that those not having a present on Christmas day had that gift to open. Some got quite emotional, and of course, that set me off. By the way, I had cooked the meal in my flat and brought it all down on the trollies that I had borrowed from the main kitchen.

On Boxing Day, I offered sausages chips and beans, and I ended up cooking for twenty-two. They all gladly paid a minimal cost for their meals and knew that any small profit would go straight back into funds for more FUN.

The year 2015 arrived, and I was making plans to book entertainers once a month for a fee of £1 per head including tea and cake. The numbers were up each month and by this time I had taken over the bingo activity as the lovely lady running it for many years was ill. I also organised 'Lucky Numbers' based on the lottery last number. Each number you bought for £1 no one else could have your number(s), I would then put on the notice board the following day the winning number that was on the TV and the person who had picked that number if any.

If nobody picked it we had a rollover. The money came in and went back out again with the exception of the rollover. This game was extremely popular. I organised a buffet for Easter which was well supported and an Egg hunt with a prize for the most eggs found which had been great fun.

Darts matches once a week with tea and biscuits. Film afternoon on Fridays, I would buy the latest films and I'd serve, ice cream, cake or biscuits with a cup of tea all for 50 p per person.

Then someone asked about us having a quiz night. They'd had one a long time ago but when the member of staff went nobody took it on, so I started that up in the evenings once a week too. It got to the stage that there were activities five days a week.

Now I don't want you thinking that I was ignoring Trevor, he too would come down to the activities most times. He would very often win at darts, loved to sit and listen to a varied range of music on music night which was from 7:00 pm to around midnight. This event too would cost 50 p and included tea and cake.

This activity was well supported as a lot of the music was of the 30s, 40s and 50s where we would all sing the songs—great fun. Within eighteen months of living in the home, I no longer had to rally the troops, all I had to do was put up the posters advertising the event and down they came.

The year 2015 for me was to be one of the most challenging years of my life. I know I have said that about other times too, but you will understand what I mean. Trevor was getting worse with his mobility and speech and eating was becoming more problematic for him, and I was trying to think of things to encourage him to eat.

A nurse came over from the hospital and showed me how to fit an external catheter on Trevor for night-time because I was helping him to the toilet several times a night, and I was so tired all the time. Although I was very involved in the activities that I enjoyed immensely, my priority was still Trevor and always would be.

Trevor had always been possessive and controlling to a certain degree and on many occasions was very hurtful. I could never chat to the chaps in the complex as he would be there making his presence known. I was also referred to as a 'foreigner' by one of the residents who had questioned Trevor's choice of wife and Trevor ignored him. I had got upset at this, but Trevor could not see why I was upset.

The resident had asked where had I been born, and I told him. He stepped back and called me a foreigner. I was hurt because I had not been called that since my school days and it upset me immensely and this is what prompted him to speak to Trevor. It's funny how some things in life never leave you no matter how hard you try.

We had maintenance people coming in and out of the building all the time, and we had got quite friendly with one of the electricians who Trevor boasted to at times about when Trevor worked in the Caribbean. The chap was around our age group and was very polite at all times as were all the staff. Every now and then, we would pass him in the corridor or as we would be going out, and he would smile and say hello.

Trevor would go off on one asking me how did I know this chap and why had he said hello to me (My dad all over again). I was so elated to think that someone wanted to greet me or acknowledge my existence and it was so nice. By now it was different with the residents as they had become like my family, my sisters or brothers and some even parents, and I treated everyone with respect and dignity, but they too, as Trevor had always done, were starting to take me for granted.

Trevor woke up one morning, and he seemed jaundiced, and I asked one of the care staff, Maggie, for a second opinion. She agreed, and I phoned the doctor. Now for months and months, I had been asking for an appointment or for a house call because Trevor was not well, but I was always put on to a locum or a trainee doctor. In the end, I think it was to shut me up the GP booked Trevor in for an ultrasound, and we got the appointment within the week.

We went in and were asked how long had Trevor been like this, and I said, "months, no really nearly a year before, the jaundice."

He was astounded that nothing had been done thus far. He was sending the notes to the GP and instructed us that we were to see our GP the following day. I laughed at him and said that is not how they do things, and he reiterated his instructions.

Instead, we were given an appointment to see a consultant in another part of the hospital if Trevor could have a stent put in to unblock a duct by the liver. Within days, we had the appointment to speak to a consultant who dealt with digestive disorders. He spoke to us about the procedure and warned that if it was cancer they would not be able to do the procedure. Within days, we got the appointment and arrived early in the morning for the procedure.

We were told what would take place. I was with Trevor most of the time even in recovery. Afterwards, other patients were being called and sent home, and we waited for what seemed ages. Trevor was getting hungry and tired and as I was getting up to see what was going on, we were called in to see the doctor in a side room.

We sat down, and he apologised and said the procedure could not be performed because Trevor had got pancreatic cancer which had spread to the liver and because of his Parkinson's they were not able to offer any further treatment. The blow for me was like a punch in the face I turned to Trevor, and we both said at the same time 'bugger', sorry for the bad language. I was stunned, shocked and started to get upset.

The Doctor said, "You honestly had no idea?"
I said, "No."

But Trevor turned to me and said, "I knew I had cancer a while back." That hurt me because he did not share this with me but then that was Trevor, again never sharing.

Within days we had to go back to the consultant to tell us what to expect and what they would do to help Trevor. Trevor was given about two to three months maximum, and towards the end, they said he could come into the hospital for palliative care. Nearly five months later on, one evening Trevor started coughing up blood and one early morning as I tried to support him to visit the toilet he collapsed on the floor, and I could not get him up.

I rang for an ambulance, and Trevor and I went to hospital A & E at Bournemouth. We went to the ward for the digestive disorders and Trevor was settled in, and we waited for the Doctor's rounds that morning to find out what the plan was. In the meantime, another patient had come in the bed next to Trevor and was very bad with jaundice and the poor chap passed away the following day.

As I mentioned before to you due to his Parkinson's Trevor had to have silk or satin fitted sheets on the bed otherwise he was not able to turn or move in bed. The hospital did not cater for this, and I was desperate to bring him home.

Days passed and Alice came to stay with me for a couple of days to see her dad and to give moral support. I was with Trevor every day from 8:30 am to 1:00 pm, home for lunch and back at 2:00 pm till 8:00 pm when I would go home and sometimes catch a Chinese meal on my way.

I would treat the residents watching the television in the lounge to a couple of bags of prawn crackers which they loved and soon got to look forward to. They'd always ask about Trevor with sadness in their eyes.

The consultant visited Trevor after around eight days and asked would Trevor want to be resuscitated when the time came and Trevor immediately said no. We had not talked about it, but Trevor had already obviously made up his mind and not mentioned it to me. By now Trevor wanted to come home and die at home.

By hook or by crook Trevor was coming home, I didn't know how I was going to manage it, but I promised him that even if I had to smuggle him out and into the car, he was coming home. Once I had told him that he would be coming home he was a bit less anxious.

Trevor was no longer able to stand or even sit in the side armchair. The staff said they did not have enough staff to help him get out of the bed regularly. Every time I broached the subject about Trevor coming home the staff found some reason why it would be difficult.

Until one day, I said that Trevor's wishes should be respected, and they said that the only way he could come home was if there were two carers assigned to him as he would need a hoist, a different armchair, a hospital bed, bedding and so forth.

So for a couple of days, I was hopping from one officialdom to another. Karen the manager did not have enough staff to spare two care staff so that Trevor could come home with a feasible care package she only had one member of staff. I suggested that I be the second carer and wheels were set in motion for Trevor's transfer to the flat.

Whilst he was waiting he became more and more possessive and anxious that I might have someone else in my life, and he could not accept that it was not true. He was putting more pressure on me. He made me feel guilty every time I left him for a break he would ask me why was I leaving him.

I knew why he was getting like that because we had spoken a couple of years previous that if anything happened to either one of us, the one left behind should find someone else and be happy and not stay on their own. I was adamant that I wanted Trevor to have someone else in his life if I went first and likewise for me. He was not happy about the comments I had made at the time.

All the equipment was delivered and the McMillan staff had brought round all the medication and dressings etc. that Trevor would need. The surgery was allocating a nurse to keep an eye on his needs when he got home. I was being turned into an unofficial nurse and our bedroom was free for anyone wanting to help us or just visit.

Trevor finally came home on a Friday morning and quite a few of the residents were sending their best wishes not really realising that he would not be with us for very long. Trevor became picky, difficult, hurtful and more and more demanding. Once again it felt like he was trying to punish me for his illness. If anything in his life was not going well, he would find ways of making me feel as though it was my fault.

He complained that I was leaving him alone in the bedroom it was only to make us tea or something to eat. I had not been involved in activities for several weeks I just needed to care for Trevor out of duty, as I had done for my parents and his.

On Tuesday, as Trevor was deteriorating Steven came to visit his dad on Trevor's sixty-seventh birthday and sat with him for some time whilst I got a bit of a break, and although Trevor was still coherent at that point, he was slipping away,

I suppose pleased that he'd had the chance to see Steven. Every now and then I would hear the flap on the letterbox and another birthday card came for Trevor. Steven went home upset at seeing his dad's condition and Alice was beside herself as she had caught a cold and was unable to see him at the end.

Trevor was constantly in pain, you could not touch him to turn him or change the bedding. All the day after his birthday, Trevor's breathing had started to become laboured and at times would stop altogether. He could not hear us anymore and was going through the last stages of his life.

My bed was next to his at night since he had come back home, and I would hear him in the night breathing. Then at around 2:00 am on Friday after he had come home I woke up with a start and Trevor was still with me. I held his hand and said, "Please let me sleep I am so very tired, truly believing that he would still be with me when I woke up. I will see you in the morning; good night, God bless."

Two hours later, I woke up with a jolt and Trevor had gone, and I just sobbed but could not bear to be in the room with him. I was scared of his body being there, I don't know why.

I rang for the night staff to come and confirm his death and to be with me. She had to ring for an ambulance to come and confirm the death and sign forms to say that. This form would be handed to the funeral directors when they came at 8:00 in the morning. I did not inform the children until that time of the morning as there was nothing they could have done.

Monica the care staff on duty that night was brilliant and so supportive. She stayed with me until Trevor was taken by the funeral directors at around 8:00 am.

On Fridays, we had a different caterer in the home, and they offered fry ups. Many more residents came down for this and there was always a buzz in the air. There was laughter, joke-telling and comments about the previous night's quiz session. I went down as usual and some had already heard the news about Trevor and were not sure what to say to me and amazed that I was not weepy or sad. I was normal and asked everyone to treat me normally and not walk on eggshells.

Trevor had passed away and was now in a better place and out of pain. I was still here to carry on with my life. Everyone relaxed after that, and we carried on as usual. This all may seem very callous to some of you but unless you had experienced all that I had and more you would not understand.

Some things I have left out purposefully particularly because I do not want to recollect them, and they would be too painful to note. Also, had I been crying all the time the residents would have also been upset and it would have been a constant reminder of their eventual demise. I felt a heavyweight had been lifted off my shoulders.

In the time I had lived at the home there had been several families who had requested that the wake of the resident who had passed away should be held at the home and asked if I could deal with the catering.

One thing I would always request—that no flowers were to be brought back to the home as residents would find this very upsetting.

All my life up until that time I knew I was destined to look after those around me. I did not think twice about it I just got on with it, if anything or anyone got in the way I had to find a way around them and forge ahead.

I knew that now it was my time to live and enjoy life as best I could. I didn't know what I wanted or needed as I had never thought about myself, and it scared me, but I knew one thing I was finally out of the cage and the commitment of sacrifices and putting myself last all the time. Basically, I had lived my life for the betterment of others, and I needed to do that for me now and find out who I really was, but I could not forget the needs of those around me, now I just had to find a happy medium.

Trevor passed away a week from coming home and two days before my birthday. I had to sleep at night with all the reminders of the last week but had already arranged for the NHS services to collect everything the following Monday.

For his funeral, I had hired a minibus to accommodate residents wanting to go. His sister Lynda and her husband and son were there. Many people from the clubs came too and the chapel was packed. I did cry as Alice read Trevor's eulogy and bless her managed to just about hold it together. Nicola handed tissues round and the Granddaughters did him proud.

The wake was held at the home and everyone came back for cake and tea or coffee. The staff should have set everything up for me to just start dishing things out, but it never happened.

Everyone was very happy at the way things went, and I was later told that Lynda's husband had made a derogatory comment about me, good job I hadn't heard him or he would not have been invited back to the home. Thank God that would be the last time I would see them as this meant that all the snide remarks and bullying would stop.

Instead of flowers, I asked the well-wishers to donate to McMillan Caring Locally and the Parkinson's group in Christchurch. Over £600 was donated to the charities. I placed a thank-you notice on the board in the home and thanked those from the other clubs personally.

After Trevor's death, I visited the staff at the hospital with Alice to let them know Trevor had passed away and to return some sheets that they had lent me for the hospital bed brought in for his last few days at home. They were sad, and I was told what a happy chap Trevor had been and always had jokes to tell them. We stood there, mouth wide open and made sure they were talking about Trevor; they knew exactly who they were talking about.

This reminded me of Alice when she had started school and had made me feel guilty. Trevor had done the same to me. I could not recollect when he had laughed at anything for such a very long time. It just confirmed to me that he had been trying to make me feel bad at every visit I made.

On my visit to the funeral directors, I was asked if I wanted to see Trevor's body and how well he looked. I had visited all my past relatives in their chapel of rest and none had any effect on me because what mattered was their sole, the body in the coffin was the garments for the soul within. I got to the door, and I asked the girl to come in with me.

I don't know why I had asked that, I'd never done that with anyone else. I got as far as the entrance of the room, I burst into tears and fled out of the room, the whole room pushed me out, I could not go near him I was even scared, but I did not know why. I was ushered out and calmed down with a cup of tea.

A while later she asked me if I would like to try again.

"No," I quickly replied. It upset me so much, I felt Trevor was pushing me away or was his soul saying you have done enough, and you do not need to see me in this way. I have no idea, but before the funeral, I tried again and asked for the lady to enter the room with me, but this time, I wanted her to stand between me and the coffin, I managed a few seconds long enough to see his body had started to deteriorate, something I had not seen in my other relatives and suddenly I had an overwhelming sadness, and I burst into tears.

When I came out it took me quite a while to calm down, but I felt that at least I had paid my respects as I had done for the rest of my family when they had passed away.

As I am writing about the fear I had at being in the presence of Trevor in the funeral parlour it brought it all back to me of when we lived in Larkfield and the spirit presence I had experienced then. I had felt the same intense fear with Trevor's body as I'd had thirty-six years previous with that lost soul in our home?

I decided to have Trevor's ashes scattered at the sea edge of his favourite beech near home. He was mad about the sea and that beech was his favourite. Both Steven and Alice came, and after our meal in his favourite restaurant, we took his ashes and in turn scattered them along the shore. It was an emotional time but a happy one too.

I soon returned to carrying out the activities and started planning for Christmas again. This time I would not need Trevor's permission or placate him so he would attend nor seek his permission to have someone visit me in the flat. Most times he would refuse, and I would remind him that I too lived in the flat, and I was not a maid or servant, and as usual, there would be no response.

Both Steven and Alice had invited me to their homes for Christmas. Knowing what I was planning at the home and the fact that I could now please myself, I did thank both of them and told them that I had a lot to occupy myself, and I would not be home alone getting miserable. Both Steven and Alice had made their path in life and enjoyed everything they were doing, but I had not, I'd had to go with what other family members wanted of me all of my life. I wanted to forge my own path in life now and for once I did not feel guilty.

The money that had paid for the order of the calendars and for Trevor's funeral was money Trevor had cashed in from a couple of small pensions when he reached retirement age. Once everything was settled with his funeral arrangements I decided to use some of that money for my own funeral arrangements as I did not want my children to be burdened with that task. I was all paid up and had no worries just peace of mind. Truthfully I would have loved a little job to keep me occupied rather than fetching and carrying for the residents a lot of the time.

On Sunday we had bingo in the afternoon as this activity was on twice a week and for over a year I had introduced 'Sunday Morning Coffee Shop', I had printed a little menu, offering toasted teacakes, croissants with cheese and ham, cappuccinos and such like and some Sunday papers were put on the tables. All profits would go for other activities.

On Wednesday we had the usual coffee morning where not many people came to but when I introduced the 'tabletop shop' selling all sorts of essentials. More residents came down and filled their rollator bags or shopping baskets, and for some, it was the first time they had shopped in a very long time and for others it saved them paying taxi fares to the supermarket, I had even offered deliveries to their flat. I was able to order shopping online and have it delivered once a fortnight.

I haven't mentioned you know who, but he was in the background stirring up mischief a lot of the time and trying to stop things that I would organise. It was a constant battle trying to keep one step ahead of him and to pre-empt his next objection.

Around eight months after Trevor passed away the whole weekly activities routine for me was losing its appeal and residents were asking for my help in lots of ways, and I just could not say no. I had no other commitments I was volunteering my time more and more. My volunteering was not just with the residents, as at the same time, I had been the main organiser for a Club with Age Concern also I was buddying for Dial a Bus for a number of months too.

I would always tell residents what my plans were for our big events, and I always tried to either break even or make a bit of profit to put towards another event later on in the year. Inviting just the residents to big events never made us any money and sometimes we had a loss, so for Christmas or autumn parties, I would make separate invitations for the people from the clubs and coffee morning groups I was still frequenting outside the home.

Due to the popularity of my events and the value for money people got, the 'outside' tickets always sold out quickly even though they were always £5 more than the resident's tickets. Usually, around twenty would come, but December 2015 proved to be the most popular ever.

I had held back the outside tickets and tried in vain to sell the tickets to residents first and at £10 for a three-course meal and two lots of entertainers of one hour each, I believed to be really good value, the party was taking place in the first week of December hoping that those going away to families would not lose out. The ticket cost to those from the clubs was £15 and everyone had thought it was really good value too.

Three weeks to go and residents were dragging their feet even though I had advertised the event with eye-catching posters. Yes, I know what you are thinking, at the back of my mind I scenically wondered if you know who was behind it, but I could not think about that at the time, I needed to sell the tickets, as entertainers had already been booked.

I decided to start selling tickets to the groups outside, once I had told them what was on offer they were fighting over the tickets, I could have sold at least another ten easily. I sold all twenty in one go. The residents suddenly wanted tickets, and with another fifteen places booked by residents, I took down the adverts at home and started planning the meals.

The rules at home were that residents had priority over those invited from outside, which was right, and I would never have disputed the fact. BUT two weeks before the event the residents were still coming forward asking for tickets and were looking forward to the event. Hold on to your hats, the final number booked to attend the Christmas Party was fifty-six, the dining area seated thirty-two; I had to have divine intervention so as not to disappoint all our supporters from outside.

I asked Karen if we could get some more tables, and in the end, we counted enough to seat all fifty-six, we borrowed tables from different rooms, dragged the jigsaw tables over from the lounge making sure we did not disturb any of the puzzles that residents were making up and as for the chairs we had the cupboard in the lounge full of chairs.

We did not have enough cutlery, crockery or glasses for the event, so with the assistance of a member of staff who used her car to help me, we went to Wilkinson's and bought all that we needed for the event and stored it all away from the kitchens. I bought table decorations, crackers, napkins. All our usual Christmas decorations were put up and numerous trees decorated.

The idea was that I would cook everything on my small cooker in the flat and bring things down when they were needed, but I found that I needed an army of helpers and the residents were not able to help. I decided with the Manager's permission that I would approach the chef from the nearby care home and see if he could help me with the cooking. To my amazement, he agreed.

Now, this is what you have all been wondering I bet, Spoiler decided to go and lodge a complaint against me to the Manager as I was setting out the tables for the party that day. His complaint was that the posters advertising the event were not up long enough for residents to be invited and that they had been taken down too soon. When I explained to Karen the situation and that all the residents who wanted to come had got their tickets and nobody was left out.

If he'd tried anything else to ruin the party, I would have to commit murder; God forgive me. After that, he kept right away and not even his pals came near us.

Anyway going back to the chef, he suggested that he would do the main meal of turkey and trimmings, and he would bring that on a heated trolley. I was to make up the starter which was either melon or pate and the desert was trifle or Christmas pudding. Everyone attending had filled in their menu choice, and I had also made place settings for all with their menu choice.

For the main meal, Chef charged us £5 per head and his time was free. I just burst into tears this embarrassed him, but he understood why I had got emotional.

My kitchen in the flat was 10' × 8' I had melons all over the place, I had brought up a trolley from the kitchen, and the chef brought a kind of sauce to go with the melon that I had prepared, the pate and French bread were plated up, and we were set to go. Now, apart from being on roller skates and running back and forth I could not have managed to wait on fifty-six people by myself. I had four rows of tables with chairs back to back and one last table for the staff and a couple of residents.

I had asked the staff who were off duty to help serve up, they all wore black clothing, and I gave them all white gloves for serving. It went like clockwork and everyone was so impressed, the staff more so.

The main meal and dessert were plated up and served as the starter. All I can say is thank God for dishwashers. The chef and his two staff were taking all their items back to wash at the home. We presented them with a very large box of chocolates and biscuits, and they were applauded and thanked by all present.

Just as the meal was being served one of the residents spotted Spoiler coming in to be nosy, and he just stood mouth wide open. When she told me I just smiled at her. Everyone coming to the event knew we were having a raffle including three hampers.

Many gave gifts for the raffle I only bought from funds some items for the hampers. Selling at £1 a strip the raffle took over an hour to call, and we raised over £125 on that alone. That money I had earmarked for our Christmas meals.

The second entertainers to sing for us were a local variety group and were very popular with the residents. The group played for a charity, the Dorset Air Ambulance. At the end of the evening, I thanked them on behalf of all those seated and reminded everyone that the group played for the charity mentioned and could they look to see if they had any small change to donate.

We counted the donations and the entertainers received over £100 plus their usual fee. They were delighted and so were we all. A most brilliant night was had by all thanks to the divine help.

No sooner than the Christmas Party was over, and I was making up invitations, event choices and menus for Christmas and this was the result of my planning for the festivities and how many came to each event—Christmas Eve (Buffet for thirty-four) Christmas Day (Turkey & Trimmings & Desert for twenty-six) Christmas Evening (Soup and a Roll & Fresh Fruit for fifteen) Boxing Day (Gammon/Turkey Chips & Beans Apple Pie & Ice Cream for thirty-one) New Year's Day (Roast Beef & Roulade/Fruit Salad for forty) Yes, all these meals were cooked and prepared by me on my small cooker. So challenging but so gratifying because organisation and planning were the keys to the successful meals cooked for those large numbers.

After the marathon meal preparations over the Christmas and New Year and not having much help from residents pushed me to make the awful decision to never attempt another mealtime like those I had just gone through. I felt hurt and a little bit used as I had done it all on a voluntary basis as a resident. The lack of help in clearing up hurt me immensely.

In spring 2016, Alice and her husband invited me to go and share a cottage with them for a week in the New Forest. When the residents heard they asked me what would they do for a whole week without me and how could I go and leave them to their own devices and so on.

I had a really enjoyable time with Alice and Darren, and I was so grateful because I would never have been able to have a holiday on my own. Alice and Darren had told Steven it would be nice if we all met up at a restaurant in Lymington to give me a nice surprise. It was a great surprise and lovely to be all together as we had not been since Trevor's funeral. I enjoyed getting up early in the mornings and walking their dog Betsie, a Springer Spaniel.

Those long walks with Betsie made me realise one thing, I was running myself into the ground volunteering. I really had to put myself first, and I knew that would be the hardest thing to do ever.

A week or so after returning from my week off and much to the delight of the residents and staff, we were all told that the Chief Executive of the Housing Association was doing a tour of three of their care home complexes and ours was one of them. Maintenance staff was around making sure everything was in working order the staff were polishing, hoovering and cleaning everything twice over to make sure everything was gleaming for the visit.

On this occasion, I also got the chance to catch sight of the smiling maintenance chap that Trevor and I had got to chat to a few times. He was with us all day checking all the lighting. I was getting fonder of this lovely smiling person.

Now I also need to say that at every event I organised even the minibus or coach trips were all recorded with photographs that went into the large albums left for viewing on the coffee table in the TV lounge. It was good for those with dementia and their families and also for those hoping to move in. On the day of the visit, the Regional Manager came in and chatted to Karen as to how he wanted the visit to be arranged.

He then came out and saw me and asked that I put the photo albums opened out on the large table by the doors to the lounge. Then he said that he wanted some residents including myself to be sitting on the sofa chairs in the conservatory where the visitors were made up of the CEO, Director, Regional Manager and Karen, and they would be expected to chat with some of us. Oh NO, we thought if Spoiler comes down that's it he will dominate the conversations and the visitors will be really cheesed off.

When the time came the visitors were all smiles, surprised at the amount of activities organised and the wonderful welcoming atmosphere they felt when entering the building. I was delighted at the feedback and some of the residents were trickling down wary if Spoiler was around. We all sat around some in wheelchairs and the CEO asked us questions which were in turn answered by residents.

I also said that the complex had been a very special place for me as it had all the facilities to help me look after my husband until his death, and I was so appreciative and grateful for the opportunity to live at the home. He was touched by the honesty residents gave in their answers. Then he said how impressed he was with the large choice of activities on offer and many replied saying it was all down to my hard work and that they were so happy at the home. The CEO praised me and said he was now going to another unit similar to ours.

I have no idea why I did it, but I slammed my hand down on the coffee table and told him that there was no need to do that as he had visited the best, and he had no need to see the rest. With that, the area manager said, "Don't say that you're going to make my job even harder."

Everyone just burst out laughing, and the visitors went away very happy as we all were.

Whilst I was away for the week I had decided that I would look for somewhere else to live, I didn't need the services of the care home and someone in greater need would benefit from my flat. The other reason was that residents were now taking me so much for granted, not in a hurtful way, believe me, they were my extended family. I owed them all gratitude for being my friends and family, for treating me like a daughter or sister. They supported me, and I supported them, but it was time for me to let go.

A few weeks after my marathon of cooking all the meals at the home, both Steven and Alice asked me if I would like to live near them rather than be alone, especially that I was contemplating freeing myself of all my volunteering commitments.

I was really grateful for them thinking of me, but I declined both. Going to live near Steven would mean that I would be the odd one out again as I had been with Trevor's family. Steven's mother-in-law would dominate what I did and where I went.

No thank you. Alice on the other hand would have loved me to be closer, and I could walk the dog and spend more time with them. That too did not appeal to me because they were very set in their ways and had forged a good life for themselves and my going up there would have changed a lot for them, and I would not be able to do what I wanted.

I'd made so many friends and was really settled in the area. I wanted to move forward and explore what life would be bringing my way. Surely I deserved that. "Well, yes you do, darling," I said to myself.

Thinking back to the beginning of 2016, a friend from the home, and I had decided we would each have a psychic reading. We travelled to and from the address by taxi as Margaret was a wheelchair user. I remember vividly being told in the reading that there was a chap at work, around me who had a soft spot for me, someone at work she repeated.

Well, that puzzled me and as I did not work I could not make it out. It was months later that the penny dropped it was my smiling maintenance chap. She had described him perfectly, but I just got stuck on the words 'at work'. Well, I did work, as a volunteer. My heart sank thinking that I would be missing out on the opportunity to find out if it really was him because soon I would be moving out.

In the summer of 2016, I told Karen that I wanted to move out of the home and give another couple the chance to benefit from the facilities that Trevor and I had enjoyed. Lettings were informed but could not help me to move into another flat run by them, I tried several times and even asked the Area Manager to help, but he could not help either. I was so upset.

Also, in the summer of 2016, I was celebrating my sixty-fifth birthday and as I had never had a birthday party what better way to celebrate it but to have a party. It would also be my way of saying thank you to everyone for allowing me to be part of their family and to also say goodbye. I posted through residents doors an invitation to my party. I had also invited all my friends from the clubs and coffee morning.

The theme was Butterflies and everything I received and every card I was given had butterflies. I bought all the food myself and prepared it all, doing a buffet was the best option. There was so much food that everyone was taking home a 'doggy' bag. Neither Alice nor Steven could make the event but were happy that it had all gone well.

The Council had been notified by the home that I wanted to move out, and they told me about their scheme of my getting registered on their housing programme and how it worked.

The local council was pleased to hear I was giving up the flat as people were desperate for this type of housing and the waiting list was long. I don't know if it was the same where you live but down south you are placed on the waiting list and you are given the chance to bid for a property you see on the council website. If your bid is successful and you meet the criteria for that property, then the council may contact you and offer you a viewing.

Now, this is no smear on the councils, their policies or staff, but in my experience, I was offered properties that were not suitable for me for as they called it 'my forever home'. My back was against the wall and the council can only put you forward for three bids if your third viewing is still not to your liking, you are then placed at the back of the queue which will take another so many years.

I was a pensioner 'widow' on benefits so I suppose I should have been grateful for the offers, but I was not prepared to take a property that would be detrimental to my future health because it was either prone to dampness and mould or was so far away from essential amenities that I would have to later on move again.

I never do anything by halves, at the same time as choosing to move home I decided to make a clean break of all my commitments and resigned from all my volunteering. The Dial a Bus was making my back worse in getting in and out of the cab.

A couple of my helpers at the Age Concern Group had moved away and responsibilities fell on me more and more. Not having a car anymore since Trevor had died made it really hard to get to the club especially in the winter.

Due to everything going on in my life and the big changes I knew that cooking a Christmas Dinner for all of us this last year was impossible. With the Manager's permission and the residents' too, I decided to approach the chef from the care home down the road to see if he could supply us with the Christmas Meal, but we would dish up. The care home manager gave the chef the green light, and we were in business.

Having got the menu from the chef, I printed up menus for each resident and the price and gave the deadline date for the menus and money to be handed in. Twenty-four residents booked the Christmas day dinner including me and everyone really enjoyed it.

Christchurch Home 4

Anyway going back to the choices with the council, I had turned down two and this would be my last choice. This next home I would live in was to be my fifth address since moving down from Horsham. I would now be viewing a bungalow in a close with seven other bungalows all for the elderly and was a mile or so away from the care home so I would be able to visit everyone from time to time. I accepted the property and my moving date was the first week in January 2017.

A couple of days after the Christmas meal in December 2016 and ahead of my moving out in a couple of weeks, the residents and staff gathered and gave me flowers, cards and vouchers/money I was so overwhelmed and surprised that they thought that much of me, I was crying so much. It made me feel guilty to leave them in order to do what I wanted.

At the same time, I was leaving my volunteer job with Dial a Bus and my much-loved volunteer job with the Age Concern Club, I had been with the club longer than I had lived at the care home, and I knew everyone very well. I was given presents and money from them too, but no amount of gifts could take away the pain and heartache I was feeling inside. It all felt so overwhelming and scary too.

Now when I said bungalow a lot of you will have imagined a really nice spacious property—NO—it was built just after the Second World War and was pre-fabricated and these properties are peppered all over Poole Bournemouth and Christchurch. It was cold, damp and expensive to heat but affordable for me to rent from the housing association it belonged to.

I was once again downsizing, and I had to get rid of more and more of my life's memories and it felt that my past was slipping into history. Perhaps that's what I needed to do now in order to move on. I offered Steven and Alice a lot of photos, family memorabilia, there were not as many as there could have been because Trevor had decided to give Steven and Alice a lot of his things before he died, he had wanted to make sure that each got what he wanted them to have and it gave him the chance to say goodbye as he did not know how things would turn out in those next few months.

So yes, furniture went too, some had to be given away and begrudgingly a lot of my craft supplies went but some I gave to my granddaughters. I was moving into a one-bedroom property that had an airing cupboard shelf for storage. It had a gully kitchen with a door to the back garden which was postage-stamp-sized and to one side the refuse bins and a side gate. The hallway was eight-foot long and the front door width.

There was a door from that to the wet room. NO don't get excited, the floor was a nonslip surface that had water stains in the corner under the wash hand basin which meant the floor was not sloping in the direction of the drain which was in the opposite corner. Using the WC was restricting because when in use your knees would be past the door opening and should you not feel well and fall to the ground nobody could open the door as you would be blocking someone from entering.

Packing and clearing out the flat was arduous and tinged with a bit of sadness at how life had been when we had first moved in. Right up to the end of December I was still running the activities all of which residents had by then got so used to Darts, Bingo, Film, Tea and Chat, Quiz, Fish & Chips delivered every Thursday, Lucky Numbers, Sunday Coffee Shop.

At the end of the year, I handed the activities and funds to my best friend and helper Sheila. Although in poor health and using a wheelchair she had enjoyed the activities so much she did not want to stop everyone from enjoying them.

The staff at the home had offered to move me and one staff member had access to a container on wheels. So between that, the two cars the staff used for loading to the roof with my belongings I moved into my first ever home on my own at the age of sixty-five.

On that first night, I had no curtains but nets so I pegged large towels to the nets for privacy and the husband of one of the staff came round the following day and hung the curtains up for me, plumbed in the washing machine and connected the cooker. Everybody had been so kind, and I was so, so grateful.

That night I sat in my new home cold and feeling isolated crying wondering if I had done the right thing. I knew deep down that it was and that I had to learn a different way of life. I had more life's lessons to learn. Over my lifetime I had experienced so many changes to my life's routine and many homes and this was to be just another, and I had to get on with it as I had done many times before.

I remember telling my children that I would only be in the bungalow until the following October as I would be moving again. They looked at me puzzled. This next October will be my fourth here so we shall see.

When I left the flat I promised the residents that I would return to visit, but I needed a month to get my head straight and unpack the large amount of boxes, many of which were plastic and were used to move our possessions from Horsham. With no spare room, they had to go, and I gave them to a staff member who had helped me.

Many of you will relate to this phobia of mine 'spiders', I do really think that prefab properties are more prone to them as I had never experienced so many, to the point that one night I spent two hours sitting on the edge of the bed crying and praying that the black 5 p sized spider in the corner of the ceiling would move down so that I could put him in my large glass and put him out in the morning (Yes, for some reason, it was always a 'him'). It took two hours, and eventually, that did happen, and I went back to bed exhausted.

My first month was excruciatingly lonely, hard work physically and very demanding at having to think about me. Who was I, what did I like, what did I want. To be quite frank from early childhood I had envisaged that the man in my life and that I would marry was very loving, and we would be very happy.

Oh don't believe for one minute that I did not have the love from my children that goes without saying, but I wished for someone to share my life with, my thoughts, feelings, and my hopes and dreams a true friend who was easy to talk to and appreciated me for who I was and who would not want to change me. I am sure many of you will know what I mean, I knew this was possible because I had heard so many friends and acquaintances say what a happy marriage or relationship they'd had.

Although I had been brought up a Catholic I knew there were other dimensions to life, freedom of choice, different beliefs. My life up until I started full-time work had been one of going to work, home school/work, church, in that order like a rat in a wheel. Then in meeting people at work and listening to their ideas and thoughts I one day decided to attend a 'church' with a work friend, it was a spiritualist church.

It was a Sunday afternoon, and I had lied to my parents as to where I would be or I would never have been allowed out of the house. Never mind the fact that I was twenty by then.

The person doing the reading at church that day was clairsentient and all I had to do was place a personal item in the basket on entering the church. She would then pick out one item at a time from the basket which was laden with many items. She would only read a few each week. She studied the piece she had picked up and proceeded to tell that person what she could feel from the item.

I had placed my watch that my parents had given me for my first communion when we were in Africa. Her first words as she picked up my watch was 'oh this is hot, very hot', and she held up my watch so the owner could identify it, but I was not allowed to say anything or be identified.

I was so taken by what I was told that it would only be me who could agree or disagree with what was being said. I knew from that date there had to be something to this side of our lives. I was told things nobody could have known specific things to my life and where I came from and some of the relatives I never knew and the descriptions were so accurate.

I only knew that from the photos I had, the information was correct and it excited me.

A number of years later, I had divulged this event to my parents and my dad was so amazed at the things I told him that I could not have known. My mum was not happy because she could not understand the process. The funny thing was that when Mum and I would have the same feeling or intuition about something, my dad would pipe up and say, "You are like witches."

"Thanks, Dad," I'd reply.

Anyway, back to my bungalow, the month was nearly up since moving in, and I was missing everyone so much I could not bear it any longer, and I rang my closest friend Sheila and asked if I could come over for the coffee morning. She nearly jumped through the phone at me and replied, "Oh yes please, everyone misses you so much."

I just cried, and later that morning, I went to see them. It was like going back to see family and such an emotional time for all of us.

I had missed them so much, even the staff were happy to see me. Everyone was saying, "Are you bored, do you want to come back?"

I smiled and said, "No, not for some time; anyway, you will get another activities person, I am sure of it."

It was a lovely visit and walking back home I went through the cemetery and it reminded me how short life really is and that I should try hard to do the things that would make me happy and those around me too.

On my own now I was in charge of my health, eating habits and exercise too. I loved cooking so everything was homemade with plenty of fruit and vegetables. With no more commitments and starting to relax I would choose places to visit by bus and made notes of bus numbers. The only horror I faced in the first few years after Trevor died was that I had to get used to walking or taking buses.

I felt so self-conscious about walking on my own. I felt that everyone was looking at me so at first I used taxis quite a bit. Then I thought if I got an MP3 and had music to listen to whilst walking it might help and it did. I was so pleased with having learnt how to use an MP3 it worked a treat and for nearly two years I did this every time I went out.

Then on a couple of occasions being in a hurry I had gone out forgetting the MP3 on the table and nearly panicked, but it taught me that I no longer needed the music, at last, I was beginning to be me.

Having my music with me gave me the courage to travel further afield. I'd take a bus to Bournemouth and jump on the next bus that came along. Residents got to know about my 'mystery tours' as they would be a source of conversation and laughter depending if I had got lost or not. Although I hated the idea of it, my bus pass had become my ticket to freedom.

Now that I was a bit more settled, still going to the coffee mornings with my other friends I asked if I could come in once a week and have the Friday meal with them all at the home. Everyone agreed and looked forward to my visit, and they exchanged gossip, mainly about you know who.

Once I had got used to the journeys and places around I got bored at having to choose where to travel to so, just like when my mum was living with us, I wrote on little post notes different destinations and folded them up and picked one on days I was desperate to be out but could not choose where to go.

Having done that several times that too got boring, so I decided with the help of Google, to choose different local places to walk to and marked the mileage from home and to each destination, and I made sure I walked at least five miles a week. Wet and windy days kept me at home as the bus stops were not that close, I did however use taxis out of desperation but only one-way trips. I didn't care if I got wet going home from the bus stop.

At times I would go out for a coffee or to the local shop with residents who travelled in their electric wheelchairs/ scooters and this was another great talking point and source of amusement at the Friday fry ups. As the residents travelled at their 'normal speed' I would have to half run alongside them.

"Are you ok?" they would shout.

"Oh yes, fine," my reply would come back with panting under tones. I do believe that this Friday event was our greatest time of laughter and storytelling—everyone was so relaxed and having fun with their favourite meal of the week.

In March 2017, residents were begging me to come back to give them some activities as there were not many because a new resident had been given the purse strings to hold and residents would have to organise events themselves. My friend Sheila was ill and couldn't cope anymore. All the residents were charged 50 p for each activity, for Bingo it was £1, and from funds, small items either food or household items were given out as prizes.

When I came back to help out the winnings for Bingo were 50 p a line and £1 for a full house. As I said I started with a couple of activities a week and Bingo was always in the evening from 7:00 to 9:00 pm.

Within a couple of months, I was back nearly in full swing. The residents had a meeting with you know who at the helm and the new manager. Spoiler was praising my return and the good work I was doing for them all. Well, you could have knocked us all over with a feather.

Most of us were open-mouthed wondering what he was up to. It was put to the area Manager Joan that I should be employed by the Housing Association, other Activity Coordinators had been employed by them in the past why not me.

The company agreed, and I applied for the job through the proper channels. My interview was at the home with the Area Manager Joan and Liz the scheme Manager as Karen had left for promotion.

It was my first job interview in fifteen years, and I was so nervous. I took in a portfolio of all my past jobs and the CV in case they did not have one to hand. The questions came fast and furious, some of the questions would be what if this happened what if you were asked to do this and similar other questions. I was really happy because I could answer everything without hesitation and many questions I answered giving examples of things I had experienced in my volunteering at the home.

After nearly two hours, I came out in a daze, and residents were hanging around the corridor asking whether I had got the job. It was a few hours later as I was ready to go home that I was told I'd got the job. I would work eighteen hours a week and times to be determined by the activities on each day. I could not handle or hold on to the money raised it had to be handed with the attendance slip to the treasurer who was a new resident. I was so glad not to have to deal with the money.

I was so happy to be able to have money to buy shoes, a coat a couple of bits for home too and most of all to relay to the benefit office at the council that I was now working and would no longer need their help thank you very much. That was such a weight off my mind.

I started my job in July 2017, and I worked my socks off. Soon I was following the same routine I'd had before I moved away. I never learnt my lesson. There was also a shortage of staff so I would help out by giving out the meals to sick residents in their flats.

I helped give residents their meals in the dining hall. Residents just could not think of me as staff and that there were lots of things I was no longer able to do for them.

It was so hard and very soon I was working nearly thirty hours a week and only getting paid for the contracted eighteen hours. I was coming home so tired that I would not eat a proper meal. Then gradually Spoiler started to rear his objectionable head again and the Area Manager was in his sights as well as me. I have no wish to go into details, but by the end of February 2018, the Area Manager, and I left our jobs in the same week because of Spoiler.

Once again everyone was so sad to see me go, but some residents could understand why and felt sorry for both the manager and me. The money they raised for my leaving gift, I added some myself and bought a condenser tumble dryer.

After a month of leaving my job, I was still applying for jobs but with no success. I thought that perhaps this time I should take a break as there was obviously a reason that I had not found another one. I had left it up until then to inform the benefit office at the council because I was loathed to go and admit that I would need their help with my rent. I was in tears giving my details and circumstances because for me I had gone backwards and was still not able to stand on my own two feet financially and to be truthful I was ashamed.

Since finally leaving the care home in February 2018, I did carry on going to my coffee mornings at the same hall where the Age Concern Group met. The lady who had taken over from me at the Age Concern Group asked if I could stand in for her when she would be away, and I was happy to do that. Then from September 2019 to January 2020, I stood in for her again, but this time, I was so glad to be finished. The weather in those months had been awful and the walk up the hill each week for some reason got harder.

Christmas 2019 was very hectic as I was still running the Age Concern Club and also I'd had to organise their Christmas Lunch at a Bournemouth Hotel plus doing everything without a car really challenged me. Then all of a sudden I'd decided that I was going to buy myself a proper sized false Christmas tree for a change and that would be my present to myself for that year. Trevor was not a Christmas person, but he loved all the food I would cook and watching the television. Consequently, since moving down to Dorset, we either had a very small Christmas tree or none at all.

I was getting really excited and keeping an eye on the prices in the shops. I wanted to make up for all the crummy trees I'd had to contend with for the past ten years, and I would go for a good one that I could bring out year after year, as I use to when the children were still at home.

Then suddenly I spotted this beautiful seven-foot plump tree in Wilkinson I loved everything about it. I kept an eye on the price; then suddenly a few days later, it was reduced. I was wondering how could I buy the tree that day as I'd already got

220

a load of shopping in my little trolley but to make matters worse (as I have told you before I don't do things by half), I decided to buy the baubles which were also reduced in price.

So there I was struggling to get around the shop and then I returned to the tree section, but I couldn't take the box to the till as I had too many things to carry. I found a young man and asked him nicely to take one of the seven-foot trees to the till for me. I got to the till and paid for all the items and got all my bags strapped to the trolley and the last one hanging from my arm and got hold of the string on the tree box and proceeded to walk out of the shop, to my horror I moved, but the tree stayed in place.

At first, I thought I had caught the box on the corner of the till and tried pulling it towards me and it still stayed in place. My brand new plump seven-foot hunk was not budging it was so heavy.

Not being deterred and with gusto, I started dragging the box behind me (all the time thinking please don't anybody who knows me see me) with a scratching noise on the ground I walked the length of the shopping precinct to the bus station end. I would never be able to travel by bus so I called for a taxi and when it arrived I warned the driver that my tree was very heavy.

On the journey home I told him my story, he could not stop laughing. He kindly brought the tree to the front door for me and said that he was going to be laughing at my story for the rest of the day well at least I made someone else happy that day.

Having moved some of the small bits of furniture to accommodate my seven-foot hunk I started assembling my giant. It took me over an hour as each full branch had to be inserted into the trunk and everything was colour coded. He stood on the coffee table and his top just below the ceiling, great I thought there would still be room for the Angel at the top.

Once I had finished I stood back exhausted and wept. It was one of the best trees we had ever had in the family, and I was so happy to have him in my home.

I emailed Steven and Alice and headed the email 'I've got a seven-foot hunk for Christmas'. They too had a good laugh at my story and asked why did I need a big Christmas tree and my reply was 'because I wanted one'.

I have to laugh though because, in February 2020, my DVD/video player of twenty years packed up. Then in March, my faithful cooker of seven years died on me. I have a feeling the cooker came out in sympathy for the DVD player. The cooker had served me very well, and I thought well I shall buy a two ring hob and sort out getting another cooker as and when I have the money.

Up till then, I had managed quite well. In a way, I was getting the feeling that I was being squeezed into submission to write the book as I could no longer view my large collection of films or cook and freeze my meals or baking. Cooking and baking have been my biggest passion so I had to find something else to create in the meantime.

Steven bless him did offer to help replace each item as they went, but I did not want that as these items are not cheap, but I did however surrender to him buying me the two-ring standalone hob.

Alice at the same time had emailed me saying that she and Darren had an old DVD player that they could post down to me. I begged them not to as this was a leisure item and was not essential and would cost them quite a lot in postage. Alice also offered to pay for the two ring hob, and I explained that Steven had already ordered me one. I am very lucky with my children and feel really blessed.

In the spring of 2020, I was all set to take over running a club for Age Concern in another part of Christchurch. I had prepared activities and quizzes but on the day that we were due to meet I got a phone call from the manager to say that until further notice all the clubs were closing.

Since being in my own little "solitary confinement" due to the virus I had thought hard about volunteering again in the future, and I had eventually decided to tell the Manager that I would not be going back to the club once the clubs were opened. If I'd started volunteering again it would have felt like going backwards and not achieving anything new.

Everything I have done in my life thus far has been for a reason and writing my 'recollections' has been for another reason too, for what that is I'll have yet to find out.

Due to the virus and restrictions imposed on all of us I had not been able to visit my old home and see my friends. Before I had left my job in 2018, I was also tipped off by Liz the Manager that Spoiler would give me a load of grief if I tried to enter the building for visits. Well, do you know what? I had by then chosen to move on and it got to a point where none of what he said mattered anymore.

Many of my friends from the home including Sheila have passed away, and I think of them often and feel them close to me at times when I am low. As for my smiling electrical engineer, I have not seen him since leaving the home, but sometimes when I spot the company maintenance vans going by, I often wonder if he is the driver in one of them.

At home I still have trouble with spiders all the time, one winter, I had a plague of woodlice and because the insulation is rubbish, in the winter before dishing up my meal I have to put the plate in the microwave to warm it up otherwise the meal goes cold before I can finish it.

All the radiators are under the windows which would be ok in a normal house, but in these prefabs, all the heat goes unless you have the radiators burning hot and worse still the windows are always full of condensation as soon as we start getting cold nights. For that reason, I try and leave putting the heating on until I really have to. What's the phrase? 'Beggars can't be choosers'.

As we all know during the pandemic the restrictions put on the over 70s was really hard. I was lucky in the sense that I was only sixty-eight at the time and with age only being a number as far as I am concerned, but I kept my outings to a minimum.

I struggled for a very long time trying to get shopping online so I would take a chance at getting bits regularly with my small shopping trolley. It was so annoying knowing that many people in my area who had cars were the ones depriving myself and my elderly neighbours in the community of essentials by panic buying or hogging the internet delivery slots. That has been the trouble in this pandemic, the selfish and the 'I'm alright Jack' meanies who have given more hardship and worry to the likes of us stuck at home in order to keep them safe.

Not having Alice or Steven live close by it's been super hard. I have bitten the bullet as they say and soldiered on like thousands of my generation and older have done too.

I have spoken to you about my Angels helping me and also my guides. For many years I have been comforted by the appearance of 'white feathers' or finding 'money'. The 'white feathers' are signs that Angels are helping and watching over you. The 'money' I was once told is your ancestors and guides who want to reassure you and help you.

Depending on my situation at the time of finding these lovely gestures; sometimes I have smiled from ear to ear and thanked them; on others, if I have been going through a very challenging period I have bawled my eyes out at being reminded that there is always someone watching and supporting.

On many occasions, where possible I have picked up the feather and placed it in my Angel box at home. When I have picked up the money, I have placed it in a glass pot and when full I've taken the money and handed it in to a charity shop.

In life, you must always try and give something back whether it is time, money or an act of kindness. If we all did that this world of ours would be an even better place to live in.

Since living in the bungalow I have now spent the past three Christmases alone doing what I want. This year I thought would be even more interesting and challenging as I would not have my cooker helping me to make all the usual delights for the festivities, and I was preparing to think of ways of cooking some of it in my microwave and slow cooker and if I was not successful then I would give up, open a bag of crisps and have done with it.

It wasn't to be, Alice rang just the other day and told me that both she and Darren along with Steven and his family were all going to pool their resources and purchase me a new cooker in time for Christmas. Hoping that you know me quite well by now, I was in floods of tears I just could not believe their thoughtfulness.

It really hit me from left field, a bolt out of the blue, call it what you like. I have to say I was just as gobsmacked as when I was told forty-six years before that I was pregnant with Steven. Wow, how blessed am I with such a lovely family?

Thank you, my darling Angels everywhere and may you too be blessed with those that you have around you.

Nicole x